OUTDOOR ADVENTURES

Bruce Wilson

Foreword by:

Sandy Lender

Distributed by
Lulu.com

Sandy Lender Ink
Beverly Hills, Florida

Outdoor Adventures
First Edition

Copyright © 2018 by Bruce A. Wilson

Publisher: Sandy Lender Ink, Beverly Hills, FL 34465

Library of Congress Cataloging-in-publications Data

Wilson, Bruce, 1950-
Outdoor Adventures / Bruce Wilson

ISBN: 978-0-9998780-9-5

In memory of
Kenneth George Wilson 3/13/13 to 8/21/1990 and
John Wesley Wilson 3/10/1948 to 9/24/1967.

Time with them in the great outdoors was priceless.

TABLE OF CONTENTS

Foreword

When you're a teenager, you have no true understanding of society and societal change. At age 12, 13, 14 and so on, I certainly didn't realize the United States was in a period of flux when it came to hunting and fishing regulation and the average person's views on those regulations, or that the flux had begun even back when I was sitting in a gray fishing boat with my dad and grandpa. (I'll take this opportunity to point out that I was always relegated to the middle seat in the boat, which will have significance when readers get to the chapter, Best Boat End. Despite that seating arrangement, I believe I still hold the record for Largest Catfish Caught by a Wilson.)

Despite the changes in peoples' points of view regarding hunting—such as outlawing young men driving trucks with window gun racks readied for afternoon sport onto school property—the average reader can still relate to stories of camping, fishing, cross-country family vacationing and, yes, even hunting. These things are not completely foreign to us yet. In this book, my dad describes something beyond the simple acts of outdoorsmanship, though. We get to see, sometimes through the eyes of a boy in 1950s Southern Illinois, a time that today's hunters and fishermen and campers have not experienced, or may have forgotten.

It's interesting to look back at the way old people did things when they were young. It also puts into perspective why my mom told my sister and me that we shouldn't refer to the rodents in our backyard as "bunnies." When Dad was going through the embarrassing trials of training a pair of beagles to recognize the difference between rabbits and mice, he didn't want to release said beagles from their travel kennel into a field with other hunters sounding his barbaric yawp: "Go get the bunnies!" We did our best to assist by referring to all long-eared creatures as rabbits whenever we remembered to…

Thus I fear this book may have its moments of angst. While the reader will benefit from that for its entertainment value, I certainly hope the reader also recognizes the importance of these stories for posterity. There are nuggets of Midwest history woven among the fun here.

- Sandy Lender

Preface

Through my outdoor adventures as a young boy, I began gathering material for this book. I didn't realize back then that some of what my family, friends and I did would one day end up in a book. Such a thought may have stifled some of the creativity that became common in our adventures.

My early in life camping trips took place before I could talk. On one of those early trips, I arose to a standing position as the moon appeared over the river; I raised both arms in awe and announced amazement regarding God's creation – using words that nobody present could interpret. Today I continue to be amazed and I write of experiences in the outdoor world using words that hopefully are more easily understood.

My father was an outdoorsman, and from my earliest memories I recall wanting to be like him. My big brother started going with Dad before me, and it was more than I could endure as I sat looking out the back door awaiting their return. Before I was five, Dad decided that I was old enough to start fishing with them. A few years later and the three of us were hunting together.

Hunting and fishing were a big part of our outdoor adventures, but there were additional types of adventures that we enjoyed. My brother and I learned to explore beyond what we knew, and we were perhaps a little overconfident as we embarked into the unknown.

During my thirteenth summer, I was taken on a combined fishing and camping trip. Only my father and I went on that adventure. Today, I understand that week was my right of passage experience. Dad let me make decisions that sometimes resulted in success, and sometimes resulted in losses. I learned, I grew, I completed the trip, and I returned home with a new confidence that survives yet today.

We grew up in a relatively small town where it was a pleasure to live. Like any town, it had its limitations and sometimes those were part of the fun of living there. With a light heart, I have dubbed my hometown as Muckville. Not exactly sure why that name came to mind.

My brother and I explored together. We took on challenges greater than the sum of our individual abilities, and our successes through teamwork built confidence. Sometimes, we learned something about our limitations. Whether our endeavor was completely successful or something less, we were happy for having done more than sit in the house. We hunted and fished together until his last days. Sadly, his last days came far too early at the age of nineteen when returning home from a hunting trip. But even in that loss, a lesson was learned about continuing forward.

My father and I continued to hunt together until physical limitations prevented his going. We fished a few years longer. Then, I hunted and fished alone except for occasional trips with special friends and family.

It is sometimes emotional to recall the 'way that it was' because we were such closely linked outdoorsmen, but life brings changes that are completely natural. Moving forward, it is still a joy to employ the things learned with my father and brother, my mentors.

Many outdoor adventures took place between the ages of eight and eighteen, and more continued into adulthood with some experiences that are hard to imagine. Memories of those times and events are as clear today as when they happened. I've put some of them on paper, complete with their special embellishments of an outdoorsman with an imagination. Hopefully, aspiring young outdoorsmen will find these stories fun to read, and possibly they will be a pleasant reminder to the older outdoorsmen that enjoyed similar experiences.

Neighbors

NEIGHBORLY INFLUENCE

Growing up in a small town and spending most of my time outside, it was essential to know all my neighbors and develop a good relationship with them. In a small town, everyone knows everyone else. This situation leads to having neighbors that tell a kid's parents anything he does that they think he shouldn't be doing. Once I realized that neighbors form a closely linked spy network, I decided that I would need to know them all. Knowing everyone provided information regarding what I could do in each segment of the neighborhood.

In the process of getting to know everyone within a few blocks of my house, some of the neighbors ended up having an influence on me. One couple that lived in the house next door was already in the neighborhood when my mom and dad built their home. I didn't arrive until several years after the house was built. Those years gave my mom and Hannah a chance to get well acquainted. Because Hannah was older than my mother, she took on the role of giving motherly advice. Mom didn't seem bothered by it because Hannah meant well. Sometimes I was bothered by the advice she gave, because much of it was directed at modifying my behavior.

The advice about my activities started while I was pretty small. I knew it started because I could hardly chase a cat with a rubber hatchet without Hannah advising my mother that it wasn't a good idea to let me run about.

I liked Hannah's husband Ralph real well. He sometimes advised me on various skills and techniques. In fact, he's the guy that showed me how to hold my rubber hatchet while chasing something.

Hannah was a good neighbor and I liked her regardless of her unwelcome advice, and she tolerated me better than most when I was at her house. I would go over to listen to her stories as she worked. I didn't know it, but I was building good rapport and trust by listening. As interesting as her stories were, watching her work was even more fun. She would string beans and other such things on her back porch during the cooler hours of the summer mornings.

I liked to get up real early, and that gave me a chance to be over to Hannah's house by the time she was outside and working. I hardly ever had to knock on her back door and ask if she had any work to do that day. An interesting thing was happening while she talked and worked, I was learning a few things. I'll not make a list.

She had a washing machine that was kept on her back porch. It seemed odd to me that a washing machine could be left outside. My mother owned something called an automatic washer, and it never sat outside. I also can't recall it ever automatically washing anything. Hannah owned one of those washing machines with the ringers for squeezing the water out of the clothes. My mother and Hannah both warned me of the inherent danger of operating one of those machines. Somehow, that made it a thing of significant interest.

My parents told me there was a danger of getting caught in the ringers. The result of getting caught in the ringers sounded gruesome, so this was one of those rare times when I decided to pay attention to parental warnings. This was not a normal practice for me. I tended to experience things for myself.

Hannah owned the only ringer type machine in the neighborhood, thus watching her was my only chance to see if the warnings had been accurate. I watched her run 3,227 pieces of clothing through those ringers, and she never did get caught in them. I still don't know if what I was told is what really happens if you get yourself in them.

Hannah's husband Ralph "Baldy" Jones was an interesting man. He had a nickname of Baldy that other men could use, but my parents made it clear to me that it would be disrespectful for a boy to call him by his nickname, so I didn't. I looked up to Ralph, and I didn't want to be disrespectful.

He worked at the Muckville City Park as a caretaker. On days that I didn't plan to watch Hannah work, I would get up and eat breakfast, ask Mom a hundred or so questions, then greet Ralph as he hurried past our house on his way to the park. He had to be there before 7:00 a.m.

Sometimes he invited me to go along, or maybe I just assumed that he had. I'm not exactly sure how that went. His days at work were so interesting that I liked being there. Between 7:00 and 7:15, Ralph and his buddy would determine their strategy for the day. Ralph's buddy was called Duty, and they didn't tell me why. Their days were nearly always the same, but their strategy sessions were held daily. While they discussed their plans, they also drank a cup of coffee. According to them, it helped them think more clearly.

I liked what I saw in their early morning sessions and filed away that memory until I was an adult and employed. I then used the same early morning strategy session each day, except that I expanded on it a little bit. I showed up early so that I could strategize for thirty minutes before doing anything. Fifteen minutes had worked so well for Ralph and his buddy, I figure thirty minutes would work much better. I'm not sure that my strategy was made better by those early morning coffees, but some pretty good friendships were formed.

Often, Ralph and Duty would start their work by gathering the litter that some of the kids left in the park. The tool they used for this was a special one, and it held a lot of intrigue for me. It was a long wooden handle with an end on it that was similar to an ice pick. Those tools were close enough approximations of a sword or lance that I had no trouble at all visualizing myself wielding one through a forest filled with bandits.

Ralph and his work buddy moved briskly through the wooded park, and within two hours they had all the paper scraps picked up within the sixty acres that served as the playground and ball diamonds. I offered to help gather the paper during several of these outings, but for some reason I wasn't permitted to touch those magnificent instruments.

I had no choice other than to resort to pretending. A long stick made an acceptable substitute. I selected a fallen limb from a tree that through a little imagination could serve as my combination lance and sword. As Ralph went through the trees to stab the pieces of paper, I followed along and served as his guard. Any bandits that jumped out from behind the trees to interfere with his work were quickly dispatched with a jab of my wooden sword. On some days, the bandits were so thick that I had to conjure up one of my horses, and ride it from one bandit to the other quickly doing in each of them. Only the horses from my stable were agile enough to keep me out of harm's way and allow me to wipe out all the bandits.

On one particular day, when the bandits were extremely thick, Ralph was in great danger. It was all my horse and I could do to get all of them. I had just wiped out seventeen bandits in a thirty second period when I sensed one on the far side of the tree. A quick side step by my horse and a lunge forward and we had him. Unfortunately, Ralph got between me and that bandit.

Ralph didn't invite me to go to work with him for a few days after that episode. He must have realized I had worn myself out trying to defend him.

Kids these days don't get to enjoy watching anyone pick up the scrap papers in the park. Ralph and his buddy have long since retired, and the new caretakers use a big vacuum device to suck up the paper. There isn't much fun in watching a vacuum work. Not unless you want to imagine a small localized tornado. Stabbing the paper scraps as they darted in the breeze was far more of a challenge.

Ralph's main contribution to my life wasn't the park cleaning activity. He gave me guidance in far more important areas of life. I need to caution here that I lived at a time when cats were often thought of as a lowly life form. That thought was prominent in my neighborhood where approximately thirty cats lived at one house. Let me say now that my feelings for cats changed later in life, but at the time of this story, they were near the top of my dislike list. I think that poisonous snakes were the only thing worse.

Ralph disliked cats almost as much as I did. I'm not sure why Ralph had the feelings he did, but it may have been something to do with his rose garden.

My dislike for cats was caused by their insistence that my father's gravel driveway was a toilet. It wouldn't have been so bad, but the driveway also served as my basketball court. Dribbling a basketball on gravel isn't that difficult after a little practice, but it is hard to concentrate on dribbling when worrying about the ball bouncing up from where a cat dropped a load.

Now that I look back at that time, I realize that we didn't dislike the cats; there were just a few of their behaviors that we wanted to modify. Behavior modification is something I studied years later while in college. I didn't know it when I was a kid, but Ralph and I were involved in a behavior modification effort for thirty cats.

I never asked Ralph why he felt the way that he did. It was enough to know that we shared something in common. He and I would sit on his back porch after he got home from work. We would watch for one of Ole Rose's thirty cats to wander into his yard. I'll come back to the wandering cats in a moment.

Ralph had a slingshot that only he could pull back. I got to try one time, but I couldn't pull it back more than two or three inches. I was impressed with Ralph's strength.

Ralph was always ready to share a story with me, and sometimes a question or comment from me would bring a story to his mind. The first time that I expressed amazement at his ability to pull back the slingshot, he spent two hours telling me about a slingshot he made when he was my size. It was made out of the fork of a tree. It had an inner tube as the rubber band. The rocks he shot in it were the size of my head. Ralph enjoyed telling me his stories, and I always listened very closely. Otherwise, I wouldn't be able to attempt to duplicate his feats.

The steel ball bearings that he shot would nearly go through the cinder blocks in his tool shed. Fortunately he never shot directly at the cats that were wandering into his garden, because it could be devastating if one of those ball bearings ever hit a cat. He didn't want to hurt them, just encourage them to roam somewhere other than our yards. That brings me back to the subject of wandering cats.

Now, Ole Rose had so many cats that Ralph and I figured we needed to alter the behavior of the entire population. We would do the whole neighborhood a favor if those cats began to stay home. We had to be careful though. Rose had every one of them named and would know if they started acting differently.

Through our attempts to relieve the neighbors of the wandering cat problem, I learned a great deal about patience and cunning from Ralph. First of all, the cats didn't just run over and line up in front of us for a lesson in better behavior. We had to wait on them to come to us and then surprise them.

Ralph's plan was to use his slingshot and safely shoot something nearby to give them a scare. If he could hit a tin can or something close to the cat, that would scare it away. At the beginning of our efforts, cats were everywhere. Over time, Ralph got a chance to make several warning shots. It became clear that shooting a ball bearing a couple of feet to either side of a cat will scare it pretty well.

Within a few days, the cats figured out what the pinging noises were. They are smarter than I initially thought they were. It wasn't long before we found ourselves waiting several days to see a single cat. Not only were the cats getting wary, but Rose was beginning to watch us. She wasn't sure what we were doing, but she had noticed a change in the behavior patterns of her cats. They were all staying on the opposite side of her house from Ralph and me. If we walked down the street, the herd of cats could be seen relocating to keep Rose's house between them and us. Eventually we declared our efforts a success and moved on to other things.

Ralph enjoyed fishing. He sometimes told stories about the size of fish that he caught when he was younger. He didn't have any pictures of the big fish. It seems that a camera on a fishing trip causes a person to only catch small fish. Anyway, fish as big as those in Ralph's past were no longer in our lakes and rivers. I guess the polluted water stunted the growth of our fish.

One summer, my dad offered to take Ralph on a fishing trip with us. Ralph was elated because it had been several years since he had gone river fishing. This turned out to be a memorable trip.

Mechanical failure brought the first bit of excitement. We hadn't gone ten of the seventy-five miles to the Ohio River when something happened that should have served as an omen. Our 1958 Chevy station wagon was only a few days old. All our fishing gear was in it or the boat we were pulling, and now there was steam rolling out from under the hood. A radiator hose had blown off the engine. Best we could figure, someone at the factory had not tightened the hose clamp.

A few hours later we were back in Muckville at the Chevy dealer. He assured my father that he wasn't worried about any damage to the engine. Just put on a new hose and refill the radiator and we could be on our way. Sure, he would repair the motor later if there was anything wrong. Dad half trusted him, so we departed and again headed for the river. It would be a few months before the trust placed in the dealer was proven to be a mistake. Everyone knows about car dealer verbal promises, so I'll not explain that any further.

We arrived at the river with enough remaining daylight to set up camp and put out the trotlines. It's understandable that the adults were somewhat tense. Ralph had all the pressure he could take for one day, and decided to go relax. He took his fishing rod down to the river bank. He also quietly took along a little brown bottle that he brought along on the trip. I wasn't certain what might be in that little bottle.

I decided that I should keep Ralph company in case he was to get a hook into one of those big fish he knew how to catch. To keep myself occupied, I took a few toys to the small sandbar where Ralph was fishing. I wasn't keeping a close eye on Ralph, but he appeared to be getting a little more relaxed as time went on. When Mom called and I went to eat supper, Ralph stayed on the river bank and continued to fish and work on releasing that tension.

Darkness was setting in and it was getting late, so I decided to head for the tent to sleep. Before hitting the sack, I scurried down to the river bank and checked on Ralph. He had decided to stay at the sandbar and fish all night. Maybe he would get another big one. With Ralph staying the night, I decided there wasn't any reason for me to carry all my stuff back to the camp.

I was up early the next morning and went to see how many fish Ralph caught. It was completely unexpected, but he'd fallen asleep during the night and failed to notice that the river came up about a foot. The sandbar was gone. Wait a minute. My stuff was on that sandbar. Ralph was in trouble, because I had expected him to watch my things.

Best I could tell, my toys could be ten miles downstream. Having lost hope for finding my toys, I figured that I might as well check to see if there was a stringer around with Ralph's big fish on it. Well it turns out that he became too relaxed and fell asleep early in the night and not a single fish was caught. That was probably good because for a moment I had thought about looking for a way to get even with him for losing my toys. Then another thought crossed my mind. There was another way to get even, but then I realized that Ralph's little brown bottle must have also washed away because it was gone.

That morning I learned that waiting too long between fishing trips can cause a person to go into a state of too much relaxation when he finally goes on another trip. It appears that over-relaxation can cause a person to fall asleep for hours, and then they may not be ready to do anything more when they do wake up. At least not right away.

I probably overreacted to the fact that my toys were lost, but I tried to be understanding as I complained to Mom. When explaining the situation, I mentioned the fact that Ralph had been assigned responsibility for my stuff. I also pointed out that I couldn't stay mad at him because he had also lost his special little bottle.

Mom must have listened closer than I thought she had. She heard it well enough that she shared my story with Hannah after we returned home. I wasn't in the kitchen when they talked, but I was close enough to hear a change in Hannah's voice that I had not heard before. Not sure what that meant.

Sadly, Ralph never went to the river with us again. It seems that Hannah always had plans for Ralph when we were going fishing. It's a good thing that I enjoyed the time with Ralph on that one trip, because there wasn't another like it. I am thankful for the one trip that we had together, because special memories were made that are still recalled after many years. Trips with friends usually end up that way. Memories get made.

Ralph and Hannah remained good neighbors and continued to have a neighborly influence on me for many years.

Pond Creek

EXPLORING POND CREEK

Our house was only one block north of the Muckville City Park, and directly behind the park was what seemed to be one of the great wildernesses in the state. It was known as the Pond Creek Bottoms. When I was in grade school, it was a vast expanse of wild territory that held countless potential discoveries. The creek was about a half mile south of our house and ran from the east to the west.

The forest extended from behind the city park all the way back to Pond Creek and beyond. It stretched from the Old Marion Road in the east to Highway 37 in the west. The wood was a great place to explore, and for my brother John and me the creek held all the wonders of a flowing body of water. The creek and the surrounding forest made an awe inspiring impression on the few taggers-along that we permitted to go with us into the great unknown.

We spent the years of our youth exploring much of the Pond Creek Bottoms, and nobody ever thought to question the name given to this wondrous place. Pond Creek. The name seems to be a contradiction. How could a creek be named a pond? Perhaps someone educated in the Muckville school system named it.

My first expedition into the great wilderness of Pond Creek Bottoms fell short of a complete survey of the area, but it did result in the realization that a journey into the heart of an unexplored area requires food supplies.

We were almost at the end of what we called the old oil well road when we decided that going any further without food would put us at a level of risk that we couldn't take. Upon coming to this decision, my brother and I immediately paused our adventure and returned home to obtain the necessary canteen of water and a backpack filled with food. Having obtained the minimum quantity of the needed supplies, we returned to our previous stopping point. At that time, it was necessary to take a break to eat a few apples and drink half a canteen of water.

Having properly replenished our energy, we were ready for a major push into the wilderness. We departed from the oil well road going in a southerly direction, crossed a small dry creek bed, and headed for Pond Creek itself. We arrived on the bank of what seemed to be a torrent of water. After staring at the water for a few minutes, an assessment of our journey was made. The hike we just completed had been a long one, and by our calculation had been several miles. Our parents would be impressed we had traveled so quickly, because we amazingly made the distance from the oil well road to the creek in about ten minutes.

The creek bank was steep and approximately three boy body lengths in height. Great care would need to be taken to prevent a fatal fall. Even if a person survived the plummet to the bottom of the creek bed, it may be impossible to climb back out.

Another potential safety concern was getting stuck in the five foot wide patch of mud that paralleled each side of the two foot wide gush of water that flowed in a westerly direction. I knew better than to get in mud like that stuff. The last time I got stuck in mud, I had to wait for my father to come pull me out of it. It's a little embarrassing for an explorer to be seen stretched as tight as a rubber band — with his father pulling on one end of him while his feet are about to pop out of a mud hole. Other would-be explorers tend to loose respect for your authority as an explorer when they witness such an event.

My brother John was two years older than me and helped me to be the first person to do many things. While we stood there at the edge of the creek bank, he offered to let me be the first to go down into the creek bed. I declined and assured him that he deserved this honor. I told him that he could be first. He thanked me with an appreciative slap on the back, which accidentally caused me to lose my balance. Once I was at the bottom of the creek bed, he thought I might as well look things over.

The water in the creek was clear, but the mud had a yellow color near the edge of the water. We decided that drinking the water wasn't a good idea. However, I was informed that I could go first if we did decide to taste the water.

After completing my investigation of the water quality, a way out of the creek bed was sought. A little ways from where I was accidentally knocked into the creek, I found a place where some tree roots grew out of the creek bank. Those provided adequate handholds to climb out.

I received some bad news once I ascended. It seems the food had all been eaten and the canteen emptied while I was out of sight. There would be little point in trying to continue without food. A joint decision was made to once again suspend our exploration of the great wilderness.

Realizing that food and water were important provisions for any expedition, we decided to better plan our next push into the wilderness. The next day at school, I was able to piece together something Lewis and Clark would have envied. My brother had likewise created a plan.

Our plans were compared and found to be a little different, but that situation was quickly resolved; my plan was modified to look like my brother's. We agreed to implement our joint masterpiece as soon as summer vacation started.

The first thing called for by our plan was a provisioning point. Nobody could carry enough food and water for a full day of exploring. It just wasn't possible. We needed to maintain a high level of energy when exerting ourselves, and that took a lot of food.

A good hiding place for our provisions would be necessary. Food could be carried to the hiding place and stored for a major push that would be made sometime in the future.

We decided that a treehouse would be perfect as a hiding place for food. At the end of the oil well road, we selected the largest tree we could find. Approximately two weeks later, we had carried enough scrap wood to the site, and completed a treehouse. Our father came to verify that it was sturdy enough to hold us and our supplies. After a quick inspection, he figured we could safely support two tons of provisions in it. It was a magnificent thing. The people from the Bounty would have been proud of us.

We began provisioning the treehouse as soon as we convinced Mom that she was better off with us exploring than at home complaining. That only took about three days. She said something or another about her hopes that someday we would have kids that wanted to explore as much as we did.

Precautions were taken early in our provisioning efforts to protect our supplies from potential pirate raids. The main line of defense was to hide our ladder when we left the area. This seemed to be working because our provisions weren't disappearing.

At first, it seemed that a relatively small amount of food would support our expedition. However, as time went on it became obvious that substantial supplies would be required. The meager supplies initially provided by our parents would never be enough. It would take some effort to convince them to provide all that we needed.

It wasn't just the food for the expedition that concerned my parents. They were also bothered by the amount of food required to support people carrying food to our provisioning point. We had by this time enlisted some "packers" to provide help in setting up our base camp. They understood their role in our expedition being very similar to the Sherpas in conquering Mt. Everest. Our packers proved to be very hungry and for each food item that we carried in for storage, a similar amount of food was necessary for eating while carrying the provision. Sometimes, it proved necessary to eat the intended provision before leaving the storage site. It all depended on the appetite of the packers and the quality of the supplies we carried. Our quantity of stored food began to accumulate quicker when raw turnips were given to us as the only form of food we would be allowed to take on our journey.

The day finally arrived when we decided that our stockpile of raw turnips was big enough for the journey. We were ready to strike out for the nearly impossible goal of Old Marion Road when bad luck hit. Pirates ransacked our supply post. Our entire supply of turnips was gone, the homemade ladder was destroyed, and a couple of boards were knocked from the treehouse. The rest of the boards had hammer marks from where the pirates had tried to knock them loose. I guess we had enough nails in the boards to discourage them.

They had come at night, when we weren't there. The fact we had been ruined by a nighttime raid ruled out the possibility of kid pirates, and we weren't able to figure out why any adult pirates would take a supply of raw turnips. The raid on our treehouse is still one of the major mysteries in my life. The only clue I ever got was that my mother seemed to stop worrying about where we were and my father assessed the damage to our provisioning point as beyond repair.

The raid on our supply post prevented us from departing on our expedition up Pond Creek to the distant Old Marion Road Bridge. It didn't mean that we gave up. In fact, it made us more determined. There would be a better chance the following year. We would be a year older by then, plus we would have a whole year of classroom time to spend planning the expedition.

It turned out that it took two years of planning, but we did eventually go on the expedition that had been so unexpectedly sabotaged. It took a lot of lawn mowing to earn enough money to buy the right kind of equipment. An army surplus back pack, army mess kit, army canteen, army leggings, army ammo belt, a special hunting knife, and a few miscellaneous army surplus items purchased at the Herrin Y-supply. These were all needed for a successful trip. We were adequately equipped.

We would need some food. Some eggs and bacon were taken for our food. We would cook those at our destination. We even took a few raw turnips to serve as a reminder of our previous attempt.

My brother John, his buddy Terry, and I set out from our back porch. Our plan was to get all the way to the bridge before we ate. After eating, we would return. At times, the temptation to stop and eat was intense. Our hunger seemed overwhelming and grew with every passing minute.

Between the three of us, we were able to maintain discipline and continue forward. We knew that if we stopped to eat, the long awaited expedition would be a failure. Eating our provisions would mean that we would have to turn back. Travelling without food at our age was ludicrous.

Resisting the temptation of food, we managed to forge ahead. The Old Marion Road Bridge came into sight as we rounded a bend in the creek. Our victory over the elements was now almost certain. Minutes later, as we walked under the bridge, the three of us felt the thrill of victory. An Olympic gold medal wouldn't have meant any more to us.

Pausing the story for a moment, I'll mention that the bridge is still there. Unbeknownst to those that drive across it, it serves as a monument to our efforts.

As we passed under the bridge, we realized that we had attained our goal. Also, there was no longer a reason not to stop and eat. A small island a few hundred feet east of the bridge was selected as a good place to build a fire to cook our food. On that day, the island was surrounded by a trickle of water approximately a foot wide, so a fire would be safer there than on the sides of the creek.

Hunger pains were starting to build and our stomachs were making strange noises. Animals in the woods probably still tell stories about the strange noises heard that day.

Regardless of our hunger pain severity, nobody could eat until a fire was made and the food cooked. Gathering firewood wasn't much trouble because Terry had never done it before. A quick explanation from John and I, and Terry had us a good supply of wood in just a few minutes.

Starting the fire was a little bit of a challenge. Nobody brought any newspaper. Thinking we might not get to eat, there were a few moments of hysteria. It started with a small gasp from my brother. That set me off. Uncontrolled noises came from my mouth and my arms made movements that meant only one thing. I had gone into perpetual hysteria. The condition was known to be brought on by many things, one of them being an adolescent boy having hunger pains.

Hysteria being extremely contagious, it was no time before it had spread and we were all flailing around on that small island. I don't have the slightest idea what got us over our hysteria, but someone finally noticed that Terry had gathered an abundance of dry twigs with the firewood. Dry twigs are good for starting a fire.

The fire was adequately burning for cooking in just a couple of minutes. Large flames that licked at the tree limbs above were good for cooking a quick meal. A good fire can be every bit as fast as a microwave oven.

It was no time at all until we had a few slices of well-done bacon. The eggs were ready in a rather short time. Eggs are definitely done when they are firm enough to act as a Frisbee. It turned out that we only needed a couple of slices of bacon and one egg for each of us. Nobody needed seconds.

Our trip back to our house went pretty smoothly until we neared the halfway point. It was about then that each of us experienced a severe hunger pain. Things would have been all right if nobody had said anything. But as soon as one of us mentioned hunger, all three knew that we were likely to pass out if we didn't eat within the next ten minutes. A frantic search of the back pack disclosed that we only had three raw turnips. We had brought them along as a reminder of our efforts a couple of years earlier.

The hunger pains were so bad that we had to choose between eating the turnips and foraging for wild food. Not knowing the difference between polk berries and elder berries, the decision wasn't real hard.

Raw turnips aren't all that bad.

Backyard Bunny

BACKYARD BUNNIES AND BEAGLES

Backyard bunnies were a rarity when I was a boy. Today, they seem to be everywhere including my own lawn. I won't get into the matter of how many I have discouraged from digging holes for their dens around my house. I'll focus this story on the effects that owning beagles can have on these pesky backyard rodents.

When I was a boy, Daisy May was our free range beagle. Freedom was something she enjoyed her entire life. She sometimes hung around our house and slept under a tree to keep cool. The postman might stop to pat her on the side or stroke the top of her head, and neighbors would do the same. When the summer heat passed and it was cool in the early fall, she sometimes slept in the middle of the road to soak up the heat stored in the blacktop. Cars would pause to let her get up and move, or they would go around her.

She was free to go behind the park and chase a few rabbits when the urge hit, or just go for a walk around the neighborhood. She had a way of knowing when she should be home, and when it was okay to be on a short journey. She was known to all our neighbors, and everyone called her Daisy.

I can't recall ever seeing a rabbit in our neighborhood when I was a boy. Rabbits lived in the fields in the country. Growing up with a fine dog like Daisy around, I didn't realize that rabbits ever wandered into town. The only rabbits I saw in my backyard when I was a boy were the few that Daisy caught and brought home to prove where she had been. Of course, these rabbits didn't really count as backyard rabbits because they lived behind the park and weren't a threat to our garden.

The world became a lot more "civilized" between the time I was a boy and today. Beagles are no longer allowed to roam freely. I don't understand why this has come to be; perhaps there was trouble with beagles being confused with German shepherds, Doberman pinschers, or pit bulls. Either that or the lawmakers couldn't differentiate between dogs with beagle-like behavior and those with attack dog behavior. It's kind of like treating a lion and a housecat the same way. Nobody in his right mind would do that, would he?

I guess one beagle can have a rather large impact on the rabbit population. Daisy was the only beagle for a several block radius in my home town, and she filed a claim on every square inch of the area. Many a day I saw her make a leisurely trip around her territory, sniffing as she went. No rabbit with any desire for self-preservation would cross her perimeter.

Most of the people in my neighborhood had vegetable gardens. They ranged from small plots that provided adequate food for each family, to somewhat larger plots like we had. I'm not sure why our garden was so big. I even mentioned to my parents that I thought it could be considerably smaller. Large gardens can benefit neighbors as well as the owner, but I can't recall the neighbors ever coming over to help pull weeds.

One of my chores was to remove the weeds. I didn't mind too much, except it seemed to always need the weeds pulled when I had plans that conflicted with my mother's schedule for me. Weeding a garden isn't all that easy. New carrot tops look a lot like weeds. Pulling weeds that turn out to be vegetables doesn't always set well with the people who planted the seeds.

Our neighbors who had gardens took care of their own. Interestingly, no gardener in our neighborhood ever suffered from rabbit damage. As I said, rabbits tended to stay out of the area. Daisy had a perimeter that she patrolled, and everyone with a garden benefitted from it. I think that even our neighbors figured out that Daisy was their friend.

Watching Daisy was interesting. Most mornings, she would get up and mosey around her perimeter. That is, unless she let a rabbit hunt behind the park take priority. On those days, the perimeter check took place in the evening.

Her perimeter was made up of a system of alleys and streets. The city had conveniently constructed the alleys well before my time. The alleys were originally constructed for travel by coal trucks, the trash man, and the sanitation man. We didn't have garbage men back then, only trash men. Every house had a barrel or tub that was used for trash such as tin cans, glass jars, and aluminum foil. Garbage such as table scraps usually wasn't put out for collection, because anything that would rot was buried in the garden. Plastic wasn't a problem, because it wasn't yet used for food containers.

Anyway, the alleys were a perfect pathway for Daisy's perimeter checks. They provided straight paths with no threat from traffic, and there were occasional places to stop for a snack. It's amazing how many people don't clean out their tin cans.

All the neighbors seemed to appreciate Daisy's efforts to keep the rabbits out of their gardens. Some of them were grateful enough to leave little bonus packs for her in their trash. Daisy was an appreciative dog, and knew when she had it good. She was careful to take whatever morsels were there without turning over the trash cans or pulling things out to make a mess. Somehow she knew to stay in the good graces of those that left things for her.

Things have significantly changed over the past thirty or forty years. Of course Daisy and even the dogs that came after her are gone. It hurts to admit this, but I no longer have any dogs. Maybe that is for the best. Today, society no longer lets our dogs be dogs. Treating them like people is not fair to them and deprives them of outdoor adventures that only real dogs can know.

I thought the world of my dogs, regardless of their abilities. I only have myself to blame for any imperfect quality in the dogs that I owned. Well, maybe that's not completely true. The breeder and trainer may also come into the picture. I'll write more about that in another story.

As for my part, taking a little more time on the day when I bought my last two beagles would have surely disclosed that something was wrong. Most likely there was difficulty during their birth, and the oxygen was cut off from their brains for too long. Their actions over a lifetime gave strong indications that brain damage existed. Regardless of that, I liked them.

It is only right that beagles like Daisy should be allowed to move freely, and at one time not too far back in history, hunting dogs were permitted to run free. Because of all the changes in the world, for the last twenty years, I had to keep my dogs in a pen. It was a nice pen, and although it was spacious, it restricted their movement more than I think is proper for a beagle. Even brain damaged dogs deserve to get to move around a little. This is especially true when a neighborhood is full of gardens that need protection. Rabbits love gardens, and without a guard beagle the rabbits will start to think the garden is for them.

During my adult life, I have not planted a big garden. I had too many things I would rather do than pick weeds. I only grew a small garden because it was the only alternative to eating vegetables that were grown in California dirt and air, which are polluted with every known substance in the universe. I didn't mention the water used in California because it's from Colorado and relatively clean. Today it's getting worse, and the conspiracy theorists believe we're being fed contaminated food from Mexico because it's cheap and grown in an uncontrolled environment. Perhaps it's time to again grow a big garden.

Anyway, rabbits started populating the cities because predators are protected in the wild, and dogs are no longer roaming freely in town. Smart rabbits relocated from the predator ridden fields to the completely dog free cities. It's a side thought, but people should be smart enough to do the same. Move from the areas where predators roam and live somewhere away from continual threat. If I didn't know better, I might conclude that some rabbits are smarter than people.

Several years ago, I became concerned that the rabbit population in my part of town had grown so large that it would affect the health of my dogs. With rabbits continually walking through the yard, the dogs couldn't get any sleep. Their eyes were bloodshot from not sleeping, and they became irritable with one another. I think they blamed each other for not being able to get to the rabbits. I hoped they would continue to see it that way.

I wasn't sure what they might do if they figured out that I was the problem.

Crazy rabbits and the leash laws cost me a fortune. After several years without fresh vegetables from my garden, I decided to see what could be done to stop the rabbits. The first plan was to put up a chain link fence around the back yard. I figured the fence mesh was small enough to stop the rabbits. Wrong.

Rabbits can walk right through a chain link fence. A really large rabbit may need to slow down and squeeze a little to get through, but to the other side they can go.

Because it was so easy for a rabbit to pass through, the fence actually contributed to an increase in the rabbit population. Any time the rare stray dog came through the neighborhood, the rabbits just ran through the fence into my yard. The stray dogs might try the same stunt, but they were too big to fit through the holes. To me, it became upsetting that a fence built to keep rabbits out was actually providing a refuge for the vegetable vacuums.

Releasing my dogs inside the chain link fence seemed like something that might help solve the problem. My dogs were big, fast beagles, and hardly anything slowed them down when they had a visual contact with a rabbit.

The first rabbit the dogs noticed was in for a surprise. At least I thought he was. As I walked across the yard to the dog pen gate, the rabbit just stood and watched. He flicked his ears a few times in a manner that told me he didn't plan to leave if he didn't want to. We'll see.

Ben and Critter had been watching the rabbit for quite some time. As I approached the dog pen, they went into their perpetual hysteria mode. By the way, perpetual hysteria can be caught by people, dogs, and other animals. It can even be passed from one species to the other.

When I opened the gate, the result was similar to opening the gates at a horse race. They were off. Out of the gate it was Critter by a nose. By the time they were halfway across the yard, they were neck to neck. The rabbit saw the rapidly approaching dogs and finally panicked, then ran for the fence.

When running full speed, rabbits can't immediately fit through chain link fence holes. They bounce off. On the first bounce, the dogs gained twenty feet on him. Ben and Critter were still neck to neck and both were committing fouls by trying to push the other one out of his way. Still at full speed and mouths open, Ben and Critter were one foot away. A split second later the rabbit squirted through a hole, and two dogs hit the fence.

Having brain damage, neither dog knew what had happened, but immediately blamed the other. The rabbit regained his composure and was sitting on the other side of the fence laughing at them. It didn't do their egos much good. This first episode convinced me that brain damage was no longer a simple possibility for my beagles.

Releasing the dogs when a rabbit was in the yard would need to be done under a better controlled situation. There was no point in creating little dog cubes by running my beagles through the fence.

Another attempt at getting the rabbits out of my yard didn't have the desired effect. Ben and Critter were having a relatively good day, and a rabbit wandered too close to their pen. Both dogs had their eyes riveted to the rabbit, and I was able to approach the gate before they knew I was around. Because our rabbits didn't suffer from brain damage and had developed some form of communication, the lesson provided by the previous close call had been passed along to all the neighborhood rabbits.

Rather than try to run full speed through a chain link fence, it is better for a rabbit to slow down and squeeze through one of the holes. Of course, this could only be accomplished safely if the pursuing dogs were delayed in some manner.

As Ben and Critter burst from the gate, it was a full bore charge toward the rabbit. At the proper time, the rabbit bolted. Right through the garden it ran, out the far side and to the fence. He slowed at the fence and slipped through a hole. Meanwhile, Ben and Critter sprinted into the garden at full speed. Their entrance was made through the pole beans. The strings, that were put up for the beans to climb, wrapped around each dog and were pulled along with them as they went through the tomatoes and cabbages. Before the dogs finished destroying the garden, the rabbit was already outside the fence.

A small mesh fence around the garden might stop the rabbits, so I decided to give that a try. This seemed to keep them out of my garden, but they still lounged in various places around the back yard. The few thousand dollars I spent on fencing created a decent garden spot and a fantastic rabbit refuge.

Ben and Critter became more and more upset with the rabbits. It seemed the rabbits realized they could sit within a foot of the dog pen. The dogs couldn't reach them, and the barking noise must have been at a frequency that didn't affect their ears. Eventually, I quit worrying about the rabbits. I decided that backyard bunnies are just a part of life.

Mining Operations

DRILLING AND MINING OPERATIONS

Money wasn't important during the first few years of life, but then I got the urge to own some hunting and fishing equipment. In the beginning I didn't need a lot, but my taste in the quality of equipment developed fairly fast. Good equipment cost a little more than I had. I blame the Herter's catalog for most of my problem, but Sears isn't completely free of blame. In fact, Sears gets all the blame for making it clear there were good, better and best grades of most items of importance.

It seems these two companies knew where I lived, recognized my needs and made a target of me. They had things timed perfectly. A catalog would show up every time I was about to get my desires in line with my ability to pay. Almost as surely, their promotional catalogs came just before hunting and fishing seasons.

There was only one option. I needed to find a way to earn more money. I couldn't sit around waiting for a government handout. Earning enough money for all that I wanted may not happen by mowing lawns. At least not at the going rate of $1.25 per lawn. Something better would need to be done.

Fortunately, I had an older brother who had similar desires to my own. It would be easier to come up with a way to make some big money if we worked together. Ideas weren't coming to mind very fast, but then fate began to work to our advantage, or so it seemed. One summer evening as dusk settled in, we were on the back porch when we heard a strange noise. Although we recognized that it was a powerful motor of some type, we hadn't heard this large of a motor anywhere around our neighborhood. When we told our father that something was going on in the neighborhood, he came outside to investigate.

He decided to take a walk and find out what was at work. Tagging along behind my dad, we walked a few blocks up the street and found a crew drilling for something. Now this was interesting. I couldn't remember ever seeing a drill rig this large, and especially not up close like this. Dad talked with some of the crew, but he made us stay back out of the way while they talked. It didn't matter. From our position, my brother and I could see exactly how the operation worked.

Dad told us they were drilling for oil. Realizing the value of oil, I thought we may need to know a little more about oil well drilling. A few days of dropping by to watch the operation was all that we needed. We then knew enough to drill a well of our own. My brother and I were in agreement that we were ready.

It didn't take us too long to figure out where we should drill. There was an oil well pump in the Muckville city park about 300 yards south of our house. The new well drilling operation was three blocks to the north side of our house. We were in the middle. There had to be oil under our yard.

A step ladder in the garage could act as the oil rig. My brother and I would serve as the power system, because we didn't own a large oil well drilling motor or transmission. All we needed was some pipe and a drill point.

Budding sportsmen that we were, we understood about improvising. An auger bit out of my dad's carpentry tools would do just fine, and there was a ten-foot-long piece of half inch diameter pipe in the garage.

It took us all day to secure the auger bit on the end of the pipe, but we got it done. Mom wasn't sure what we were up to, but our efforts kept us busy in our own yard, and so far there was nobody hurt or complaining. Whatever we were doing was probably okay.

The next morning we were back to the work and began drilling. This activity did bring an inquiry from Mom about why we were trying to drill the pipe into the ground, and we didn't give a real clear explanation. When in the oil business, it's best not to let a lot of people know what you are doing. If word got out, we could have neighbor kids start operations in our alley or along our front street. We wanted this to be our effort. We didn't need interlopers or help. What we earned on our own, we got to keep. Of course, we didn't yet know about the IRS.

When Dad arrived home from work that evening, we had the pipe most of the way into the ground. He wasn't real surprised to see a pipe sticking out of the ground. He had grown accustomed to finding something new around the house when we had a whole day to work on an idea. He did ask about the pipe and I guess he saw the striking similarity between our drill rig and the one up the street.

At first, we thought our drilling operation had come to an end. Not only was our father acting a little skeptical, we were running out of pipe. After some bargaining in the form of our begging and pleading, he decided to finance our operation. Oddly, he didn't negotiate his share of the expected profits. I guess that he figured it was better for us to be working our own oil well than to have us go up and bother the people at the other drilling operation while they were working theirs.

Dad was a machinist and could get materials for cost, so he bought us some more pipe. He even made a T handle to mount on our oil pipe. The new handle made the pipe much easier to turn and we were able to put his pipe wrench back with his tools.

Several more days of effort got the pipe another few feet into the ground. Our progress may have been slowed by bringing the pipe up to check the drill point for signs of oil. We checked it quite often because that was what they seemed to be doing on the big rig up the street.

After several days of drilling on a dry hole, we got a break. We stopped by and questioned one of the men at the big rig. He called a couple of his buddies over to join our conversation. They gave us a few pointers about drilling. It seems that while drilling an oil well, you sometimes hit water before the oil is reached. Sludge (mud) on the drill tip could be a good sign. At least, that was our understanding.

One evening we were drilling after dark. Then it happened. We got the sign we needed to encourage us to go on. We brought the tip out and it had mud on it. We were sure that we were finally closing in on success. That night, I started having visions of the new semiautomatic Remington that I would buy with my first oil sales. Mr. Peak down at the sporting goods store was going to be a happy man when he saw me.

The mud was a false omen. Two more weeks of drilling never did turn up any oil. Even though we went down a whole fifteen feet, we didn't get a thing other than a little mud. It started to make sense after the guys with the big rig failed to hit oil. Just our luck, we had been getting advice from people that didn't know what they were doing. We closed down the Wilson Oil Exploration Company.

Our outdoor sporting plans had not changed, so there was a continuing financial need to be met. We needed another venture that had good potential. Oil wasn't the only way to strike it big in our part of the country.

There were coalmines all around our town. They were numbered. Number 9 was east of our house, number 15 to the southwest, number 2 to the northwest, number 11 north, number 18 to the northeast. There were two old mines along the south edge of town that had already closed.

Every day, trains filled with coal from the active mines would pass by only two blocks from our house. One car load of coal would probably finance a few years of hunting supplies. Perhaps we could get in on the big money the coal mining companies were raking in.

All the mines within a twenty-mile radius of our house were shaft mines. That meant that strip mining was out of the question. We would need to sink a shaft. Digging in the yard had been outlawed by our parents for several years, so we needed another location. Pond Creek was a good place. We could save some digging time because the creek bed was already about ten feet deep.

A decision was made to let our friend Happy in on the mining operation. One more person would speed us up. We agreed to let him have 10% of our earnings. That seemed fair because we were the founders of the mining company.

We decided to use a slope shaft because we couldn't afford the elevator required for a vertical shaft. The mine entrance was placed about halfway down the creek bank. That would save us five feet of digging and still be high enough that the creek shouldn't flood our mine.

The start was a little slow. Each time we dug a few inches, some of the roof would fall. The result was that we were creating a five foot deep trench in the side of the creek bank. We kept working assuming that we would eventually overcome the cave-ins.

After a few days of effort, our parents began to wonder why we came home each day covered in dirt. Not that dirt was unusual, but a complete coating was something new. We were questioned some, but our answers remained vague. Just digging holes. If Happy hadn't been allowed to participate, they would have continued to wonder until we hit coal. But, Happy, the blabbermouth that he was, couldn't keep quiet about anything. He mentioned the Wilson Mining Company, and my mother at first thought it was amusing. Then he mentioned the shaft was a little soft and kept caving in.

Our mining operation came to a halt until Dad could evaluate our work site. Happy decided to go home when he saw our reaction to having to stop our work. We weren't too thrilled about having to discontinue a project that was a sure thing.

When dad arrived home, Mom made sure that she told her version of what was going on before we could attempt a reasonable explanation. She made it sound as though we were trying to kill ourselves. No matter how much we insisted that our operation was safe, Dad was going to be required to check us out.

We took him to the Wilson Mining Company, Mine Number 1 entrance. He was real impressed. At least he said that he hadn't ever seen anything like it. My brother and I were as proud as any two miners in Franklin County.

Our father was a wise man. He gave us several lessons on how we must proceed, and gave us specific work rules. It was easier to comply with the rules than to take the risk of having our company liquidated. Progress slowed significantly because of the new rules for operations and safety. We were young, but it gave us a compassionate understanding of how the other mining companies felt a few years later when OSHA came into place. If enough rules are implemented, an operation can be completely stopped.

We were required to reinforce the roof with a continuous layer of wood and support it with side posts every foot. Today, when I see the news on television showing the tunnels under the U.S. / Mexican border, it's like seeing the shaft to our first mine. The labor involved in transporting the materials to the shaft was enough to wear us out. By the time we would get to the shaft, we were too tired to dig for more than a few minutes.

After working a couple of weeks under the new rules, we were only three feet further into the creek bank. Our math skills were already quite well developed, and we checked with the local miners about the depth of that first vein of coal. By our calculations and based on our progress, we could expect to reach the coal in 21 years. By that time, the coal companies would have it all removed. Realizing that bureaucracy had tied our hands, and that our sporting equipment purchases were planned for the near future, we abandoned Mine Number 1.

Eventually, we gave up on the idea of striking it rich with an oil well or coal mine, but we kept looking for another opportunity. We still needed to earn enough to purchase one of those fancy guns.

Maybe we should write a book.

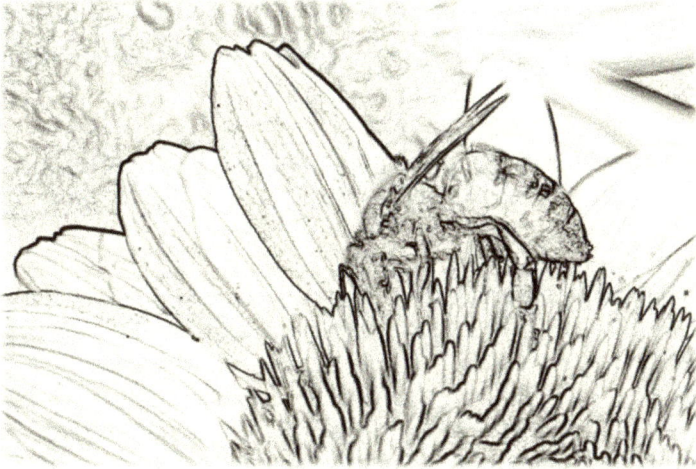

Busy Bee

BEES

Nellie, my wife, has a passion for bugs. Cockroaches bring out this passion in a way that anyone can recognize, but a flying bug with a stinger transforms hate for bugs to what most psychologists would label hysteria. Bees, bumble bees, wasps, hornets, or yellow jackets all cause approximately the same reaction. There's a shriek, a sudden gasp for air, flailing arms, and skid marks left by her sudden departure.

My reaction to bees is considerably different because of some experiences from my childhood. After several years of dealing with honey bee attacks, I learned that the best thing to do is to stand still and let them sting. When they get tired, they'll leave. Now this same advice would not be given for those killer bees that recently moved into our country. I didn't grow up around them and have no advice that would be of value for that particular insect.

Our yard was full of clover when I was a kid. Some lawn keepers hate the stuff, but I found that clover was nice. Sometimes I could find a four leaf clover, which I had heard was for good luck. Those little clover stalks with the white or purple bloom at the top, they could be pulled up and tied together to make a little rope, and the rope tied into a necklace. Girls liked getting those.

It wasn't just me that thought the clover in our yard was nice. All the honey bees within ten miles of our house thought the clover in our yard was good stuff. By the time I was ten years old, I had been stung approximately 1,382 times. Individual stings aren't that bad unless they are on a tender part of your body or happen at an inconvenient time.

I made the little league baseball team during my tenth summer. We were known as the Bombers. Coach Arms was unemployed, so he had the team practice every day except game days. He must have been a good coach because we were undefeated that year. At first it seemed odd that he had us practice in the middle of the day, but it turned out to be pretty smart. Practicing in the middle of the day made us a better team than the kids that practiced in the evening. It wasn't that the heat of the day made us work harder. It was simpler than that.

Muckville City baseball diamond number 2 had a swarm of wasps that took up residence in little burrows they dug in the infield. I played first base, and within a five-foot radius there must have been thirty or more dark holes that went down to wasp dens. It seems that each den had room for ten or twenty wasps. In addition to playing first base, I was our relief pitcher. Approximately the same number of dens was located near the pitcher's mound.

Wasps come out of their dens when the sun is real hot. Because we practiced during the heat of the day, the wasps were always buzzing around. The kids who practiced in the evenings missed both the hot sun and the wasps.

I think the wasps were a major contributor to the success of our team. Wasps appeared at random times and from random locations. That had a tendency to keep me alert, and it had a similar effect on the rest of the team. Being alert is important to a baseball team. Come to think of it, if my teachers had known about this, they could have used a buzzing sound to get back my wandering attention. Yelling wasn't working well for them. I'll need to address my problems with teachers in another story.

After a while, it was almost possible to predict the hole from which the next wasp would emerge. Placing a foot over the hole would delay his appearance. Careful foot positioning could close multiple holes. That cuts down the odds of an unexpected wasp getting in on the next play. It also increases the odds of irritated wasps in the area following a play that pulls me off my position over the holes.

Playing first base requires some agility and concentration to avoid making an error. Making an error wasn't in itself all that bad, but any error resulted in an immediate lecture from the coach. Nothing was much worse than having the coach explain how to do things correctly. Coach could take an hour to explain anything. As an example, he spent at least an hour at every practice explaining the proper standing position for a good defensive infielder when waiting for the pitch. He kept insisting that we all be still and concentrate. It really bothered him to see us jump around. He never did understand all the quick foot motion between pitches.

Watching the Bombers make a play on the ball was especially interesting to the uninformed observer. Our glove motion was different than that used by other teams. We learned our technique by trying to scoop the ball off the ground without raking a glove across a wasp as it exited from its hole. Wasps don't like that.

After a few practices and 52 wasp stings, the rules the wasps imposed on our use of ball diamond number 2 became very clear. Don't bump a wasp while it is coming out of its hole. Don't stand on a wasp's hole for more than five seconds unless you plan to move approximately thirty feet immediately after moving your foot. Don't rub your legs together to scratch any itches. Watch 28 holes at the same time for emerging wasps.

Our infielders came up with a rule of our own. Should a wasp be in the path of a ball that has been hit in your direction, time the catch so the wasp is caught between the glove and the ball. This kind of thing really improved our timing. It also reduced the risk of a wasp sting. Don't use this method for bare hand catches.

On game days, our team didn't have practice, so I had some time to fool around in the clover patch at home. When facing an evening in baseball shoes, a barefoot walk in the clover is a good way to relax. The cool clover peddles against my toes really felt good.

My mother was hanging laundry on the clothes line when she jinxed me. She used the 'D' word. She said, "Don't be running around here barefoot, you'll get bee stung." After dodging wasps coming out of thirty holes in the ground, I thought my alertness and agility had improved enough there wasn't much chance of another honey bee getting me in my own yard. Having learned to deal with a swarm of wasps while playing baseball, I figured that I knew enough to avoid being stung in the clover patch at home.

Darn! Trick bee. Under the clover leaf where he couldn't be seen. Boy, that hurts.

The ball of my left foot was rapidly increasing in size. My mother wasn't giving me much sympathy, and there were only a couple of hours left until game time. If mom had only avoided using the 'D' word. Every time she said, "Don't do something," she caused me to get hurt.

As game time approached, I somehow put my baseball shoe on my swollen left foot and headed to the park. I road my bicycle to avoid walking on my throbbing foot. Once I arrived at the ballfield, I had to get off the bike. When I hobbled up to the coach, he gave me some good news. I had been hoping for this all year. Today, I was going to be the starting pitcher. Seems our normal starter had taken an unannounced leave of absence.

Sadly, this wasn't a good day to get the big break. After three warm up pitches, I asked that the second backup pitcher be sent in. My left foot was really hurting when I landed on it. I'm right handed, and a right handed pitcher doesn't have much fun when he has a bee sting on the ball of his left foot. Try it sometime.

Coach gave me his sympathies and mumbled something as he sent me back to the mound. He said something about toughing it out for seven innings.

My parents were there to watch. Mom thought the coach was unreasonable, but he was the coach so I should give it my best. I ended up pitching all seven innings. That little ole bee sting resulted in some strange pitching motions. The pithing was not that accurate, but the unusual motions appeared to throw off the timing of the batters. Somehow, we won that game, but that one little bee sting sure made my first pitching experience painful. I think it could have all been avoided if Mom would have avoided that 'D' word.

Getting stung by various insects in the bee and wasp families over the first several years of a person's life causes a level of growing dislike for the bugs and ever increasing desire to get revenge. I knew that someday, I would get even. My dad was observed using a method of wasp nest removal that I thought would be appropriate for the revenge that I needed. He used one of our old cane fishing poles to reach up and knock a nest from under the eaves on our house. When I saw this, I knew that I had the knowledge to eventually get revenge.

Wasp nest removal was a fairly simple process, but mastering it has some risks. When I walked up behind my dad the first time I saw him remove a nest, he didn't notice my arrival. He was perched on one leg, much as a sprinter at the start of a race. An arm was stretched toward the wasp nest to direct the pole to the base of the nest. A short movement of the pole knocked the nest free and it fell to the ground. Immediately after the nest came loose and far before it hit the ground, my father streaked past where I stood.

As the nest continued its plummet, twelve supersonic wasps passed. They were on the same path my father took. He went clear to the shed before he stopped. The wasps gave up on him and were headed back my way. That was the day when I first came to clearly understand the meaning of a beeline.

This first wasp nest removal lesson was complete and it got one clear message across to me. Flip the pole, then run like crazy. If they do fly past you, do not stand around and wait for them to return.

One day after school, my friend Burt was telling me about a monster wasp nest on the house next door to where he lived. I suggested he tear it down to make sure he didn't unexpectedly get attacked someday. Burt said he didn't know how to get the job done without getting stung. Since he didn't know how to accomplish the job, I volunteered to go to his house after school and demonstrate the process for him.

Burt didn't do as much fishing as me, so he didn't have an old cane pole to use. Being a learning outdoorsman, I already knew how to improvise. We would simply find the longest pole-like instrument in his neighborhood. The longest thing we found was a broom handle. That could be used in place of the cane pole.

Burt wasn't sure it was long enough, but because I was the expert I assured him that it was. By stretching while standing directly under the wasp nest, I could easily reach the nest. Of course, this position would require that I move rather quickly when the nest was flicked from its attachment.

Carefully positioned, poised to move quickly, a flick of the wrist, and the race was on. An immediate sprint of thirty yards was almost enough. Upon stopping, two wasps buzzed by my head. Another thirty yard sprint and I stopped again. No stings. Success? Not quite. Burt said the nest had not fallen.

No problem. Wait for the wasps to settle down and try again. Using a little more solid stance, I was sure to be able to get a hard enough whack at the nest to knock it loose. I knew that I needed to be careful though. A solid stance would result in a slower start for the sprint.

A quick movement of the broom handle, and the sprint was again in progress. After fifty yards there were still wasps around my head. At about seventy yards it was safe. No stings. Success? Not quite. Burt again announced that the nest had not fallen.

It took a long time for the wasps to settle down. Burt thought he had learned enough about wasp nest destruction. I assured him there would be no problem and that the lesson wasn't complete until the nest was down. By this time his mom was outside giving advice. She used the 'D' word. "Don't you boys get stung."

The third attempt brought down the nest. My sprint had been delayed by the rock solid stance that was necessary to clobber the giant wasp nest. I had taken two steps when three wasps decided to get even. I sure wish Burt's mom hadn't said anything. I was done with my wasp nest removal actions for the next few years, and I never again used a broom handle as a nest removal tool.

Wasps and bees don't just hang around houses. They also like barns.

My sister's horse Billy had a dislike for bees that is similar to that of my wife Nellie. Because Billy didn't have any arms to flail around during his hysterical fits, he flung his legs. After witnessing a couple of his outbursts, it became apparent that I should do anything possible to prevent a bee from getting close to him.

During one of my horse riding visits at my sister's farm, a bumble bee decided to harass Billy while I was saddling him. It came out of nowhere. Buzzed in and slammed against Billy's neck right in front of my eyes. There wasn't much choice. Get rid of the bumble bee, or get a close look at flailing horse legs. Billy's eyes were already searching for what had tried to fly through him.

Being a quick thinker, I just used my hand and brushed the bumble bee away. Not liking to be brushed off, the bee turned and came back to the spot he had just left. Billy's eyes were big, and hysteria was about to set in. Hysteria being a catching kind of thing, I was beginning to come down with my own case of it.

Not being able to think during a fit of hysteria, I grabbed the bumble bee with my hand and flung him through the air. Having wings, he didn't seem to be bothered a great deal. He simply flew back and this time landed in my hair. At the time I had really thick hair. Billy was about to get over his case of hysteria until mine got real bad. At that time Billy caught another case from me.

It was hopeless at this point. We were involved in a case of exponentially increasing perpetual hysteria. Mine would get worse, causing Billy's to get worse. As his got worse, mine would get worse. If we could have found a way to use the energy levels we were developing, Muckville wouldn't need a power plant.

Neither Billy nor I were ever stung by that bumble bee. I have figured out a few possible reasons why we didn't get stung. One is that we were running so fast that the bee was blown out of my hair and he couldn't catch up with us. Another possible reason is that the bee caught a bad case of hysteria from Billy or me and couldn't get his stinger to work. But most likely, the reason was that nobody said something like, "Don't get stung."

Family Boat

BEST BOAT END

It is amazing how a person can forget all he ever knew as he enters adulthood. Something can be as obvious as the nose on your face, and yet an adult will overlook it as though it didn't exist.

A prime example is the best end of the boat from which to fish. Any kid that has an older sibling and father to go along on his fishing trips can tell you that a best end of the boat definitely exists. Of course, the father can never understand why the boy thinks there is a best location in the boat, because he is an adult and has already forgotten. Although he has forgotten, and swears the boy is making things up, he fishes from one end of the boat.

I was six years old when I figured out that there is a best end of the boat from which to fish. My early observation was made when my father, brother and I were fishing in Horseshoe Lake, near Olive Branch, Illinois. We worked our boat through the Cypress trees with the greatest of care as my father caught monstrous bluegills. They were so large that when we returned to camp and showed them, the other men felt inept as fishermen.

My brother was hauling in an occasional bluegill that made even my father envious. One of them, when fried, filled a paper plate. I had a worm on my hook that was about to start collecting social security checks.

The problem was obvious. I was in the middle seat. My father and brother were at the two ends of the boat. Any kid that has fished from the middle seat knows that the two ends of the boat are far better fishing locations than the middle seat.

The excuse for the seating arrangement was that I was too small to scull the boat or run the outboard motor. This reasoning seemed adequate at first. As time went by, I noticed some problems with the reasoning that was still being used to position me in the middle seat.

Not once did we run the motor while we were actually fishing. Our fishing excursions usually included about five minutes of motor running and eight hours of fishing. As a side thought, it is amazing how my father and brother caught fish without ever owning a 150 horsepower outboard motor to continually move us from one end of the lake to the other.

Let's get back to the seating situation, the reasoning, and the excuses. Seldom did a sculling paddle slip into the water. The person in front may never need to lift a paddle. We mainly pushed our boat through the trees and logs by gently grabbing limbs and brush as we moved along. The foot controlled trolling motor hadn't been invented yet, and would have gotten in the way if we had one.

Because we never used the motor while fishing and didn't do much paddling, I began to suspect there might be another reason I was sitting in the middle of the boat. When I asked about this, I was given more logical reasons for my seating location. The anchors were located at the ends of the boat, and I was too small to manage them very well.

This reason seemed adequate and I again accepted what I was told until I was six feet tall and able to convince everyone that I could finally handle the anchors that had been getting bigger every year. There was something about the winds in the Midwest. It seems that each year they would get a little stronger, requiring a larger anchor to hold our boat in place when we had located a large bed of bluegills. According to the other men in my family, the anchors were always a little larger than I could quietly handle. That came to an end when I stood a few inches taller than either of them.

There is no doubt that the middle seat in a fishing boat is by far the worst location. If you have never fished from a boat and are someday invited to go, the depth of the friendship should be questioned if you are assigned the middle seat.

The person in the front (called a bow) of the boat usually keeps the boat positioned to fish straight out from the bow. The person in the middle can't fish any new water without reaching across the front person. Reaching across a person is certain to cause questions to be brought up about your fishing ethics. There could even be talk about whether or not there was a mix-up at the hospital when you were born.

The person in the back (called the stern) of the boat will sometimes accidentally turn the tiller in a direction that causes the boat to swing around sideways. Another ploy is to slip a paddle in the water under the guise of helping the person up front. In reality, with the slightest of movement the paddle is used as a rudder to swing the boat around, providing the person in the back with access to new fishing water that even the person in the front of the boat can't reach. However, the person in the middle can't reach anything at a time like this because the middle of the boat is likely to be against the trunk of a Cypress tree. On the occasion when the middle person can get his line in the water, there is little hope that it is in water that hasn't seen the bait from at least one of the people at the ends of the boat.

The solution to the middle seat problem is to get old enough and big enough that nobody in the boat is bigger than you. This will result in getting to select one of the end seats.

There is something very strange about selecting the end of a boat for fishing. No matter which end of the boat you select, it is going to be the wrong end. It might seem logical to let the other person select their seat first, but this isn't really a good idea. They are certain to select the best seat.

My first fishing trip at the back of the boat was memorable. The front of the boat was always positioned to permit the front person to fish all the new water. The back of the boat was in a position to put the middle person between the back of the boat and the really good fishing locations. The only open water to be fished was directly behind the boat.

No fish in its right mind would let our boat pass over it. Not with the middle person tapping Morse code signals through the bottom of the boat. It was obvious. I had been stuck in the back of the boat on a day when everyone knew the front of the boat was going to be best.

I finally got the front of the boat on what appeared to be a good day. As we started out, the air was still and the temperature was mild. We were at a lake that had no trees, which meant on that day the front person needed to be ready to scull. Ten minutes after starting to fish, the wind picked up to about fifteen knots. Not too bad for a sailboat. Our fishing boat seemed to act like one.

My arm began to ache after three hours of trying to keep the boat off the shore. Attempting to maintain the correct distance from the shore resulted in the boat pointing from the shore at an angle of about 60°. This is perfect for the back person and middle person to fish the shoreline for bluegills. Struggling with our boat in a 15-knot wind makes it impossible to fish even a simple bluegill rig. With the temperature skyrocketing to 95° by 10:00 a.m., the front seat turned out to be less than expected.

Any kid can tell you there is a best seat in the boat, and if you want to know the best location to sit in, just ask the youngest member of your party. The kid will almost certainly point to a distant seat. It is just as certain that another person will be sitting in it. It might even be you.

If you don't have a kid with you, try the question on a kid in someone else's boat. Care should be taken in asking this question, because as soon as the subject is brought up, the kid may cause some turmoil in that other boat. Additionally, I'll point out that the best location in that kid's boat may not be the best location in your boat. Things aren't that simple.

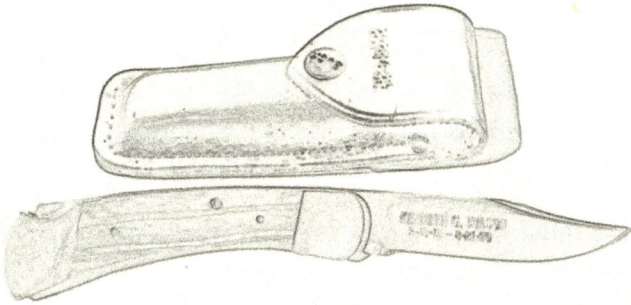

Prize Knife

KNIFE TRADERS

Any boy acquainted with the outdoor adventures knows the value of a good knife. Even though knives were originally invented for cutting things, they come in handy for a variety of other tasks. A real big knife can be used as a hammer, and a very small one can be used to clean your fingernails. If you're real steady, one could be useful for removing a splinter. Knives have great utility. Without a knife, it would be hard to survive in the wilderness. No outdoor sportsman would be caught without one — except at school and in airports.

Regardless of its intended use, the process of obtaining the knife is an art form. Of course, there are some people who simply walk in a hardware or sporting goods store and buy one out of a display case. That is a sure way to pay too much. Recently I saw what looked like $20 knives in a display case and they had price tags on them for more than $150. People that buy these have fallen prey to modern marketing techniques and aren't really knife traders.

Each knife trader develops unique rituals for buying and selling. Depending on whether a trader is looking to purchase a knife or planning to sell one, the trader's behavior will be quite different.

When looking to buy a knife, the trick is to get the seller to offer you a deal without ever indicating that you are interested in buying. If it is revealed too early that you deeply want the knife, it will cost more.

Of course, the opposite is also true. When selling, it is imperative that no prices be mentioned prior to the buyer indicating a desire to purchase or barter for one of your knives. Prematurely communicating that you want to sell will result in a lower selling price.

Because of the hesitance to admit what either party wants, it can sometimes take days for a couple of master traders to put together a deal.

Our neighbor Bob was a knife trader. I've mentioned him elsewhere in regard to trading firearms. When it comes to knives, Bob's main interest was in what he called collectors' items. All his knives looked like old junk to me. I guess it's true that one person's junk is another person's treasure.

As I grew up, I too became a collector of knives. I wasn't interested in the type of knives my neighbor Bob had. Mine all had practical uses — like scaling fish or skinning rabbits.

My first knife was given to me by my Grandpa Broy when I was about five years old. I can still remember when he gave it to me. I was on his front porch trying to learn how to fly. His porch was a few feet off the ground, and I thought I might be able to fly if I tried hard enough. They tell kids that in school now. "If you want to be something badly enough, anything is possible." Flapping my arms in the air must have made my blood circulate faster, because as I flapped I began to feel light headed. Feeling light, I thought that I may actually be able to float. When I felt light enough, I would jump off the porch to see how far I could go.

Grandpa came out and asked what I was doing. When I explained, he gave me a rather curious look. He was pretty old and may not have realized that anything is possible if you try hard enough. After looking at me for a while, he turned and went in the house. In a moment he came back out. He told me to sit down beside him.

He explained that he didn't think that I would be flying too far, and might possibly get hurt if I persisted. Knowing that I didn't give up easily, he offered an alternative activity. Out of his pocket came a pocket knife. My eyes protruded from their sockets only a short distance, and I could still see the gleaming new knife just fine. It had black handles with a rocket ship painted on each side. It looked like one of those Buck Rogers space rockets.

Grandpa said the knife was mine to keep. I had to promise to be careful, which I quickly did. A short lesson in whittling was given, and I was ready to start carving out masterpieces. Grandpa said that one important part of the lesson was to be sure I didn't whittle on anything that grownups wanted to keep. Remembering that advice would keep me and him out of trouble.

Being only five years old at the time, I knew enough not to brag to my parents about my new knife. Mom didn't understand as much about boys as my grandpa. She might want to put away my knife if she became aware that I had it. Best thing to do was keep it in my pocket except when Mom wasn't around. Well, someone told my mom. It took some begging, but Mom and Dad agreed that I could keep it in my dresser and I could get it out when I needed to use it.

As amazing as it was, I never did cut myself with that knife. My luck wasn't as good with others that I owned. I probably wouldn't have ever cut myself with any knife if it wasn't for my parents using the 'D' word.

I was making some moccasins from a few scraps of leather. As I poked holes in the leather with my knife, my dad warned, "Don't be using a knife to do that, you'll cut yourself." Well, I had been doing just fine up to that moment. Within five seconds of Dad uttering the 'D' word, I had a gusher going from my left index finger.

Pocket knives are pretty good for carrying around, but owning a sheath type hunting knife was absolutely necessary if I was to be seen as a real hunter. It seemed that everyone had a hunting knife except me. I was patiently reminding everyone of this fact over a two- or three-year period.

Our neighbor Ralph worked at the Muckville City Park. He let me be friends with him and he would listen to me talk about things I did and things I would like to do. He knew about my desire to have a fixed blade knife, and one day he brought home a knife that he found while at work. At least, he said it was a knife. It was a rusty hunk of metal that was shaped something like a knife blade, but the handle was gone. He offered to let my dad have it to fix for me. Something was said about trying to bring peace and quiet back to the neighborhood while retiring a particular topic of discussion.

Dad managed to polish up the blade and make a handle for it. The balance wasn't much for throwing, so I had to use it for cleaning fish and skinning rabbits. That knife was not exactly the one I had imagined, but it was adequate for my hunting and fishing needs. At least, it was adequate for the time being.

There was a negative aspect to getting a free knife. Getting a knife in this manner doesn't provide any experience in knife trading. You also don't get to pick the knife that you get.

It wasn't too long before I realized that an outdoorsman has needs that require special purpose knives. I didn't know there were special purpose knives until other knife owners at school provided insight into the importance of having several knives. Best I can remember, Mr. Peak down at the sporting goods store also provided some of my education on this subject.

Before my first deer hunt, I decided that I should have a special knife for field dressing a deer. Having mowed lawns all summer, I managed to save several dollars to use for hunting equipment.

I went down to Peak's sporting goods store. He had all kinds of knives. The one I thought that I needed was about twelve inches long and weighed as much as my shotgun.

For some reason, Mr. Peak didn't think I needed the "big" knife. He steered me to some knives that he thought were ideal for deer. He showed me the most expensive one first. I didn't have that much money with me, so he explained that it wasn't really perfect for deer hunting anyway. As we worked our way through the display cabinet, we finally found the perfect knife. Wouldn't you know it, the price was only a little less than the amount of money in my pocket. It was my lucky day — either that or I was beginning to get some experience with knife trading.

My new knife looked good hanging from my belt. I hurried down to Mamie's Sweet Shop to get a soda. Mamie's husband Joe usually ran the place and always enjoyed me making a visit. I was often there. As I reached in my pocket for a dime, I accidentally caused my knife to bulge out where one of Joe's new customers could see it.

The man asked me if I had a new knife. Joe winced and three people got up to leave. I handed Joe the dime for my drink and began telling the new guy about my knife, the way I had buffaloed Mr. Peak into selling it for a fantastically low price, and what I would use the knife for during the rest of my life. I am glad that I told him all about it when I did, because I never saw that nice man again.

By the time I was in high school, I had all the knives a person could possibly need. However, I didn't have one of every brand or model. One thing in particular that I didn't have was a good quality small pocket knife.

One day, while in freshman English class, I noticed Burt behind me cleaning his fingernails with a pocket knife. This took place during an era that occurred a long time before sharp instruments of any size were feared and prohibited in schools. It was a Case folding knife about two inches long with two blades. It was just the type thing I needed for whittling whistles out of tree limbs.

The teacher was busy talking about diagramming sentences, so I had time to talk with Burt about the knife. He was willing to show it to me. After looking at it a few seconds, I handed it back. I explained to Burt that I didn't see much use for a knife like that. A hunter needed something a little sturdier.

Burt couldn't help but agree that he didn't have much use for it either because he was a hunter. When asked why he had it, he responded that he had been meaning to sell it. Of course, it would be hard to sell a knife that no hunters would have a use for. What did he think he could get for it? *A dollar.* Never happen. *Seventy five cents.* Not likely. *Fifty cents.* I have fifty cents. Thanks Burt.

I used that knife for ten years before it was lost on a fishing trip. That means it only cost me five cents a year for the use of that knife. My life hasn't been the same since that loss. It really hurts to lose something when it was obtained through a carefully executed deal.

While in college, I had some car trouble that I couldn't repair myself. I took the car to a repair shop that was located way on the other side of town. When I dropped the car off at the shop, I had to walk home. It was a hot day, a scorcher, so I decided to stop off at a lumber yard at midtown. It was one of those old lumber yards with the potbellied stove and a few old wooden chairs inside. Fortunately, the stove didn't have a fire in it. Usually there would be a couple of old men in those chairs, but they weren't around that day. The overhead fan was slowly turning. A man in bib overalls saw me walk in, and he came over and asked if he could be of help. He probably wasn't expecting a college age knife trader that day.

I explained that I only needed to cool off a little. Perhaps I would look around. Over near the corner was a glass display case with Old Timer knives in it. "Say, mind if I look at the knives?" The man walked over and suggested that I might hold a few of them. Hmmm, he wants to sell a knife.

The first one felt just right. Three blades were perfect for whatever I might want to do. The price was right. I had that much money with me. There would even be enough change to get a soda out of the machine. Getting the right knife for the amount of money I am carrying is a special knack that I developed. I took that knife home.

My supply of knives is adequate for the types of hunting I do, so I am not looking to buy another. Not that I wouldn't buy another knife if someone needed to sell one.

Unfortunately, I'm not even sure where a person goes to make a knife deal anymore. All the knives I have seen in the past several years have been in display cases with a price tag underneath. The stores have their prices set so high they are embarrassed to let the general public see them. You have to ask to see the price. Once the price is set, that's it. Nobody is willing to haggle over price or even try to figure out what kind of knife fits my budget. I can't remember the last time someone asked me how much I was planning to spend.

Maybe I need to go out to a small town and see if a store like Peak's Sporting Goods is still in existence somewhere, or check to see if there might be an old lumber yard that sells loose hardware. If I find one of those, maybe they still make knife deals.

Mountain View 1962

VACATION 1962

    I thought I was the luckiest kid in the world for many reasons, and one of them was that my family took a vacation almost every summer. I don't know how my mom and dad budgeted for it on my father's income, because he was a machinist and didn't earn a lot of money. There must have been a few things that we did without during the year to make sure enough money was saved to make a vacation possible. That and it probably helped that we kept our costs to a minimum while on vacation.

    When we were at middle school age, my brother and I didn't fully understand the magnitude of the efforts our parents made to take us on vacation. Sometimes our behavior was a smidgeon less than perfect, and that probably distorted things such that it looked like we were a little unappreciative. It wasn't our intention to make it look that way or for it to be that way. We simply had not thought that deeply about it.

    Our vacations usually included some element of outdoor adventure. Because vacation time was always in the summer, we did some fishing, camping, or picnicking during most of our trips. One year was extra special. We planned to travel by car from our hometown of Muckville in Southern Illinois all the way to Seattle, Washington. We intended to fish once we were in Seattle, and there would be several opportunities to picnic as we crossed the plains and the mountains.

Muckville had a few thousand people, and although it was pleasant enough place to live, the town itself didn't have a lot going on that was very exciting. The big excitement was a Friday night football or basketball game. When football and basketball seasons were over, people had to look for things to be excited about or to include in their idle time conversations.

When word got around that our family was headed to Seattle, there was a lot of talk about how we could ever afford such a trip. Money wasn't the only concern. They had no idea how we could find our way to such a distant place. Why, the interstate highways weren't yet built and the existing two-lane highways were not directly linked between our town and anything near the northwest. Actually, we weren't linked directly to anything more than about 100 miles away.

The concerns of the townsfolk kept them busy asking questions. What they didn't understand was that our family had three master planners, and a mother, to ensure success. Among our planners, two of us were young explorers that had already been throughout the Pond Creek Bottoms, so there was no lack of confidence in our family.

My father was the only one with a driver's license, and there would be a lot of driving. The estimate I heard was 2400 miles. Wow! That was a long distance even for us. Because we wanted to make the cross-country drive to the mountains as fast as possible, we thought it would be a good idea to take along a second driver. When one driver was tired, the other could drive for a spell. My cousin Zeke had a driver's license. Maybe he could go along. Zeke liked to drive fast and that would help us get across those plains states.

In addition to my cousin Zeke, there was another family member that was beginning to slip into the planning. It wasn't in my plan. It wasn't in my brother's plan. It wasn't even in my father's plan until my mom and sister worked on him a little. Now, I loved my little niece, and it was fun to play games in the house with her, but she had been working on a characteristic that came out anytime she had Grandma (my mother) around. From the time she was about four she started perfecting her ability to wrap her grandma around her little finger. She was now eight years old. That meant she had been improving on her abilities for four years.

My niece was named Tessie, Tess for short, Terrible Tessie when she had her uncles upset. My sister wanted her little girl to have a chance to see the nation. That was not in itself a bad idea, but the way it came about raised some suspicions on the part of two uncles that were somewhat inexperienced at fulfilling the role of being a supportive uncle.

The idea of Tessie going with us was mentioned to my parents at a time that neither my brother nor I was within hearing distance. It was a brilliant strategy. The deal was made, and Tess was now in my mother's and my father's plans for the trip. There were six people going on a 2400 mile journey in July and riding in a 1962 sedan that had no air conditioning.

Unbelievable as it was, our sister and parents had slipped one past us. My brother and I only objected halfheartedly, because we knew there was no hope of changing anyone's mind. We did occasionally drop a few subtle hints.

After some contemplation of things that may be needed on our trip, we asked for permission to take along some rope and tape. We wanted the rope in case some road pirates had to be tied up, and some tape would be useful if something needed to be mended. It didn't work. No rope, no tape. Tessie went on the trip and we had not one thing we could use to control her movements or stop the jabbering. Jabbering was in 1962 what young boys called it when a little girl attempts to say more than a sentence or two.

My father had two weeks of vacation time, so we decided to leave on Friday after he got home from work. The plan was to drive through the night until we arrived at our aunt's house in Iowa. If things went well, we would be at her house by midnight and get some sleep before heading west the next morning. We had been to Aunt Lil's new farm only one time, and that was in the daytime approximately three years earlier.

Iowa looks different at night, when all the roads are in trenches between rows of eight foot high corn. Every corner appears to be identical. After two hours of hunting for our aunt's house, sometime around 2:00 a.m. we paused to update our plan. Good planners are adaptable.

Because we had seen Iowa before, and Nebraska didn't hold any magical appeal to us, we decided to make a dash for the mountains. Drive all night and all the next day. Rotating turns between our two drivers, we could cover much of the distance across the plains states. At the end of that first full day, we would stop for a night's rest, and then make another all-day drive in an attempt to get to the mountains. Nobody wanted to stop for anything in Iowa or Nebraska anyway.

The night went pretty well. Tessie slept. The night air was cool enough that a couple of windows open about two inches kept everyone comfortable. Although it was suggested that everyone but the driver should get some sleep, I couldn't do it. I couldn't sleep. If I slept, I would miss some of the night scenes. Even though we're talking about the flatlands, there still could have been something worth seeing and I didn't want to miss anything.

Morning was interesting. Sunup was behind us, but it was nice. We stopped to eat breakfast at a small place in a small town. Everyone was awake when we stopped, except Tessie. Waking a little girl from her beauty sleep isn't smart. In Tess' case, it seemed that anything less than twelve hours of sleep made her a little cranky. In spite of my brother and me trying to get everyone to leave her asleep in the car, she was taken in the restaurant with us. She would have been fine in the car. It was 1962 and the crazies had not yet expanded into small towns.

After breakfast, we filled the car with gas and were on our way. With a full tank of gas and everyone fed, my father figured we were good for about 300 miles. But then, he was used to travelling with two boys. This trip would be different. Ten miles down the road we stopped to let a little girl go to the bathroom.

The morning sun was getting rather warm. Sitting in the back of a west-bound car puts the sun on the back of your shoulders. I suggested opening the window a little more to circulate more air and cool my back. The idea was agreed to by my big brother, and we both rolled our windows down. A gush of air came in, and an onslaught of complaining began like you would expect to hear when a politician is told that he is behind in an election poll.

Tess didn't like the air blowing her hair. Some dust came in the window and got on her face. A bug flew by and scared her. There seemed to be only one solution to what we saw as the problem. Sometimes, perspective can make a huge difference in what the problem appears to be.

Two boys placed their hands over her mouth to keep her from talking so much about the things that bothered her. To our surprise, on and on she talked although not very clearly.

The muffled noises she made seemed to upset my mother. Mom made us turn loose of Tess and roll the windows up to the point that a few molecules of air might come in if we all sucked in a breath at the same time. It became so hot that it would no longer be necessary to stop to cook a lunch. We could put the cooking utensils on my shoulders.

Speaking of lunch, for that we stopped at one of those roadside tables and Mom made us some sandwiches. It didn't take long to prepare a few sandwiches and eat, then back in the car we went.

To prevent heat stroke, it was necessary to imitate the techniques I observed birds using when they are hot. They spread their wings to keep from holding in too much body heat. That's what I did. My brother liked the idea and did the same thing. With our elbows spread from our bodies, Tess seemed to think we had encroached on her allocated space. Another onslaught of complaining began and our last hope of remaining cool vanished.

By mid-day we were going through a city that had larger buildings than anything I had seen in previous travels. Fortunately, my sister gave my brother and me cameras for Christmas, and we both brought them along. In fact, my brother was entrusted with my sister's movie camera and a couple of rolls of film. We were budding photographers as well as hunters, fishermen, and explorers.

I managed a couple of quick photos through the front window and was coming up on the best possible angle of an interesting building. Tess produced a camera from somewhere, announced that I had to get out of her way, enlisted my mother's help, and moved into position to take the picture I had seen first. It appeared to me that some sort of competition had begun.

After all this, she asked to be shown how to take the picture with her new camera. Nobody in the back seat knew anything about how to use her particular camera. That must have been an automatic competitive photographer response or something. But I lost that particular competitive event. I still have photos from the trip, but there are none of the architectural wonders that I hoped to get on film (film was used before digital cameras).

The end of that first day came and we stopped at a motel for the night. We had no reservations and we passed several motels with no vacancy signs. Finally, we found one that had rooms available. We were lucky. It was near a small river that my brother and I briefly checked out. We were so tired that we didn't even attempt to fish. Tess was pleased about the choice of hotels. The bathroom had pink tile in the shower and cashmere bouquet soap. I still don't know what cashmere bouquet soap is, but it makes girls happy.

Off we went the next morning with hopes of reaching the Rocky Mountains. We weren't looking for anything special as we passed through the very small town of Murdo, South Dakota, but my brother saw a sign that caught his attention. The sign was in front of an antique cars museum. Once he announced his sighting, the two of us pleaded in such perfect unison that it must have been pleasing to the ears of our father.

For the first time in our lives, our father upon our request turned the car around and headed back. He took us to see The Pioneer Auto Museum. It was as if though we had wandered across the automotive archive of all time.

For two boys that loved cars (budding mechanics and drivers) it was as though we were in one of the great wonders of the world. The owner was a really nice man that took us through some of his displays. He even had a trick box for me to look in. It was supposed to have a rattle snake in it, but you will need to make a visit yourself to find out what was really in there. I wouldn't want to spoil anyone's experience by exposing the secret here.

After a thorough visit to all areas of the museam, back into our car and off to the west we went. That same day we made it through the Badlands of South Dakota and arrived at Mt. Rushmore. We stopped for another night before entering the Rocky Mountains.

Zeke hadn't been allowed to drive very much before we got to the mountains. That was probably a mistake. We were taking the two lane highways through the mountains because the four-lane highways weren't built yet. Zeke thought the curves presented a challenge and an opportunity to improve his driving ability. He gradually increased speed to the point that I was holding onto the seat. I left finger indentations in the material that never did go away. My father had Zeke stop and they went to have a little talk.

My brother John loved to fish, even more than I did. I wanted to get to Seattle and fish in the Pacific Ocean. John didn't care where he fished. Anytime we stopped to eat a picnic lunch, or stopped at a hotel for the night, he would usually have his rod out of the car and be at the nearest pond, stream, or lake. After eating, we would try to round up everyone and get on the road. John's usual reply was "just a minute." I don't think any fish were ever caught on one of these extra minutes, but that didn't reduce the effort put into trying.

I spent my time doing a little exploring when we made a stop. All kinds of things can be found at a roadside picnic area. Many of them I didn't recognize and my parents thought I should stay away from unrecognized objects, bugs, or animals. No explanation, just don't pick it up if you don't know what it is. Such rules can sort of take the sense of adventure out of a roadside stop.

When the mountains were finally reached, things improved. The air was cooler, and the scenery kept me busy. Watching for bears and other wild animals is a full time job. Didn't see any bears until we passed through Yellowstone National Park. Saw plenty there. This particular trip took place back when people fed bears and as a result those bears were plenty brave. Brave may not be the correct word. Perhaps bold, or aggressive feeders, would be more appropriate. We had been warned so didn't feed the bears, but I thought one of them was going to eat one of us.

We were having a picnic lunch when three bears came up to see what we had. No, not those three bears. Strict instructions had been given not to feed the bears, so we pulled Tess to the car with us as we ran from the approaching bears. I'm glad that we didn't have time to think longer about it. We may have done something we would later regret. Mom would sometimes say that. "If you do that, someday you may regret it."

Much later in life I heard something about bears and personal safety. *"You don't need to outrun a bear to survive. You just need to outrun the slowest person."* It's probably best we didn't know all there is to know about surviving a hungry bear attack. I'm pretty sure that Tess was the slowest in our group.

Well, everyone survived what later became known as the bear attack. The six of us continued onward and eventually we made it to Seattle. We spent time with my father's sister and brother-in-law and their poodle Babette. They took us everywhere, and I rode in their 1962 Thunderbird. That was a thrill. We saw the 1962 World's Fair, went to Mt. Rainier, and dug clams on the Pacific Ocean Beach.

We stayed in Seattle until we knew our travel time home would put us at the end of Dad's vacation, then we headed home. The return trip to Muckville was going to be just as long as the trip to Seattle. Two of us were learning a lot about our little niece and she was learning to deal with two uncles that were sometimes less than completely understanding of her wellbeing. Several events occurred that probably made her wonder if she would survive her uncles, and a few of them caused me to wonder if I might end up living without a niece. With most of those types of events in the past we were doing pretty well together, yet there were those moments that created a little tension.

We made one of our roadside stops to eat lunch, and I noticed the sunlight reflecting off something on the side of a nearby hill. The hill was actually a huge pile of shale and rock pushed out of a mine. There was no doubt about it, the hillside was glittering. GOLD!

I didn't have time to eat. It was time to go exploring. Full speed I ran to the hill and up the side of it. I grabbed a hunk of that glittering rock. It was about a fourth of an inch across. Darn, I had seen that stuff in school. It was fool's gold. Didn't matter, it was better than nothing. I gathered up several pieces and took them back to show my brother. He was so impressed that we both went back for more.

Tessie was whining to come along, but we quickly told her that it was too dangerous and just happened to say it loud enough that Mom would hear. It worked. My mother wouldn't let her go. She was warned of a potential fall and slide down the hill if my brother and I weren't able to protect her. I didn't completely like the implications of that comment. It felt like I was judged before I had a chance to take any action. Fine, I could live with it if Tess stayed behind. We had a mission to complete.

I found the biggest piece of fool's gold in the U.S. It was an inch across. Maybe a little more. My brother was impressed. He was trying to trade me several small pieces for my one giant piece. That wasn't going to happen. This rock would impress everyone in the Muckville Middle School. They might even think it was real gold.

My brother and I were assaying our take as Dad drove away from the picnic area. I had learned by this time that little girls want to have fun and have a strong desire to possess shinny rocks, but I didn't yet understand the extent to which they will go to get those things. Tessie decided that we should split our treasure with her, and my mother agreed. With some reluctance, it was agreed that we would give her a few pieces. The large pieces were put in a pile for the rightful owners, and a few small chips were put in a pile for Tessie.

An overwhelming urge must have come across her. Her hand shot like a bullet to the monster sized nugget that I had such huge plans for, scooped it up, and put it in her mouth. I couldn't believe it. That was a boy trick. Where would she learn a thing like that?

All holds were off at that time. I was in the process of prying her mouth open when it happened. The twit bit down on the nugget. A twit is the same as a little niece that causes your eye to twitch and causes sudden desires for getting retribution.

Fool's gold is very fragile, and the nugget in Tessie's mouth shattered into dozens of small pieces. I was as crushed as that rock. I can't recall the exact words my father used to chastise her, but a change took place in those few moments.

Tessie knew she had crossed the wrong line. Not a lot more needed to be said. Tessie realized that my brother and I now had permission from at least one parent to keep her at bay. There was a lot more cooperation over the next 1500 miles. I might even say they were enjoyable.

We all arrived home safely, including Zeke and Tess. Interestingly, our relationship was not damaged and now the trip can be recalled with joy. I have portrayed, as accurately as I know how, the events of this wonder filled trip, but I wonder if Tess might tell a slightly different version.

Ready To Hunt

ENOUGH IS ENOUGH

Some sportsmen think the amount of equipment you own has something to do with your status among other sportsmen. I don't agree, because I am a practical kind of sportsman. I belong to the school of thought that says the experience while hunting and fishing determines a sportsman's status. It just so happens there is a connection between the amount of equipment a sportsman has and the kind of experience that takes place. It seems that each year, there is a change in the amount of equipment needed for a truly meaningful experience.

I have always received satisfaction from feeling that I am successful as a sportsman. Success has in part come from knowing when I have the minimum amount of equipment for whatever sport I participate in. At just about any time in my life, I have also known the next fifteen or twenty items I need to become even more successful as a hunter and fisherman. I've seldom put these items on a written list. Creating a written list introduces the risk that someone will discover that list and perhaps build a strategy to curtail my enthusiasm. Someone may even come to an inappropriate conclusion that once those items were obtained, that would be the end of it.

The value of items on my list has varied over the years. When I was a small boy, they were things available at the surplus store known as the Herrin Y-supply. If the supply store didn't have it, I could probably find someone willing to sell their used items to me. The Y-supply was in a neighboring town, so getting anything from there required that I get my father to take me. He wasn't always in a mood to spend a day letting me browse the store. As I began earning some money, I discovered that Peak's Sporting Goods carried new guns, knives, and accessories. Most of their goods were a little pricey for a boy earning money by mowing lawns, but I could walk there or ride my bicycle. I came to know Mr. Peak pretty well. He understood my needs and served as an encourager.

I believe that my needs were kept reasonable and that I never pursued an excessive amount of hunting or fishing equipment. My brother would agree that my needs were reasonable, my dad only found it necessary to provide a minimal amount of guidance for some purchases, and Mom sometimes rolled her eyes. I never did figure out exactly what Mom was trying to communicate, but then I sensed that I shouldn't pry too deeply into her feelings. Now, as a happily married man, my wife occasionally asks why I need something, but she doesn't make a big issue out of it. Usually I can stop explaining my reasoning within an hour or two. I know to stop when she leaves the room.

After a few decades as a sportsman, I've reached a point where I am very near being adequately prepared. I don't need a whole lot of additional equipment. At least not that I am aware of at this moment. That could change the next time one of those Herter catalogs comes with all those new gadgets that turn the sporting world on its heels.

Speaking of catalogs, I've been noticing that the normal seasonal books don't always get to me. Now, I know they are being sent because I have funded a large part of the sporting equipment industry, and they would not overlook me. My wife has assured me the postman must not be getting them in the correct mailbox, but that seems a little odd. I'm guessing, but it could be that one of my neighbors is getting to my mailbox before me.

This all started out pretty small. Prior to my first rabbit hunting season when I was a boy, I accumulated nearly enough equipment to start the season. Old clothes no longer suitable for school would suffice as my hunting clothes. My slip over boots that I normally wore to school on rainy days would be used to keep my feet dry. Only ten items to go, and I would be ready for hunting. One gun and nine shot shells would set me up fairly well. That isn't too much to need. One gun. A few shells. Some old clothes. Things worked out. I had the clothes, a hand-me-down single barrel shotgun was loaned to me and a few shells were provided by my father.

I was eight years old, so the offer of using my uncle's old gun was quite attractive. It wasn't one of those sissy 410 gauge pop guns either. It was a twelve gauge. All the guys at school would be impressed. I already knew that impressing my buddies was important. Even though I didn't need much for that first season, it was important that among my classmates the correct impression be made with whatever I did get.

By the end of that first rabbit season, I developed a needs-based list of items for the following year. A replacement for the gun that kills at both ends was high on my list. The hand-me-down kicked so hard that I developed a flinch that would take ten years to get over. Two genuine hunting boots would keep my feet a lot warmer if I also had two thick hunting socks, one for each foot. A hunting coat would be a must. Not that I had yet proven a need for a game bag. Twelve shells would be needed to fill the coat — six in each pocket. It's not a big list. Only eighteen items in all. I wish that I had thought of gloves.

1	gun
1	hunting coat
2	hunting boots
2	hunting socks
12	shot shells

Quality criteria had not been established for my first year equipment needs. That led to a few experiences where I discovered that I would in the future need to set criteria, albeit somewhat loose criteria. The replacement gun should kick less than the 12 gauge. A 20 or 16 gauge would be fine. I still needed to avoid those little 410 pop guns. Boots that briars don't pierce would be good. My hunting boots should be the green rubber kind that real hunters wore. My hunting coat needed six shell loops in each pocket and a game bag, a large game bag. I planned to actually get rabbits the next season.

Our neighbor Bob Childers seemed to know when someone wanted to trade knives or guns. He showed up at our back porch at about dusk one evening. He had the prettiest Steven's single shot 16 gauge that was ever made. Under the porch light, there was no doubt that this gun was meant to be mine. Sixteen dollars was all he wanted, and I had managed to save that much from a summer of mowing lawns. Strange how the price was the same as the gauge and also the same as the amount I had saved. Maybe it was a sign or an omen of some kind. Dad looked it over and gave me the okay to buy it. I don't think I was ever happier about a gun purchase.

Dad bought me some hunting boots that year, but the hunting coat was going to wait until sometime in the future. Not having the coat with a game bag didn't turn out to be a problem, and I carried a few shot shells in my pockets.

The 16 gauge kicked almost as hard as the 12 gauge. It was hard to concentrate on aiming when the anticipated kick was running around in my mind, and that meant the rabbits weren't being seriously threatened.

I began working on a plan to further reduce the recoil of my hunting gun. That beautiful little 16 gauge was going to be good trading material for the next year. Perhaps I would look for a pump or autoloader. Something a little heavier would not kick so hard, and three shots would give me a better chance against the trick rabbits that lived in my part of the country. All I needed for my third year was a new gun, a hunting coat, new boots because my feet grew, new socks, and maybe a new knife. If I started getting rabbits, I would need a knife. The rule in our family was that if you shoot it, you clean it. Again, I had not thought to include gloves. Not sure why that kept happening.

1	gun – pump or semiauto
1	hunting coat – 6 shell loops per side, game bag
2	hunting boots – green, briar proof
2	hunting socks
12	shot shells
1	knife

The gradually changing list of items doesn't indicate that I needed a lot of additional items, and although some of the items look like duplicates of previous purchases, they weren't. Growing is a natural thing for a boy and that alone requires replacement of certain equipment. New boots every year is only logical if you are a growing boy, because the old ones get outgrown. Socks tend to wear out and must be replaced. Even the hunting coat is limited to a couple of years usage because of growth. It just so happens that replacing these items because of growth does open up the possibility for upgrades. A word of advice to the young sportsman is to take advantage of the opportunity to upgrade when growth takes place, because that opportunity will only last until somewhere around the age of eighteen.

In my case, I've found that guns can require replacement for a number of reasons. Abilities or needs can expand beyond the capabilities of the present gun. Besides, getting another gun isn't really a new item if the old one is traded for the new one. It's a replacement, or at most an upgrade. It usually takes a seasoned hunter to grasp that logic, and I've found there is little point in attempting to explain it to the non-hunters in my family.

The equipment list for the fourth year was again, not very big. I needed to trade for the pump or autoloader mentioned earlier, get a coat with a game bag that will surely be needed with the new gun, and get a knife. Of course, new boots and socks are again needed and one box of shot shells. Notice that maturity has resulted in counting shells by the box instead of individually. Later in life I will use the same counting method for duck decoys. Decoys should be listed as one dozen instead of twelve.

As can be seen, the first four years of hunting proved that I was not greedy. I never wanted more than was absolutely essential.

By the time I was twelve, an important aspect of hunting was becoming clearer. A minimal amount of new equipment each year could accumulate into quite a respectable inventory if nothing was traded or thrown away. This approach to acquiring equipment required a little more creativity and mowing a few more lawns, but achieving the status of an adequately equipped sportsman ranked fairly high on my list of priorities.

Anytime new equipment was purchased, the items that would normally be traded must be considered as retired or assigned a specific use. This change of status resulted in the new item being considered a replacement rather than an addition.

If allowed only a few new additions per year, it is necessary to use the "retirement" of some equipment as a means of accumulating all the things necessary for diversifying to hunt more classes of game. The reclassified items may be used to hunt specific types of game. If something is retired, it should be a policy that it is permissible to occasionally hunt with the retired piece of equipment to keep it in working order.

Although I developed a well thought out policy for acquiring the needed equipment, many years went past with only a minimal arsenal for all of my hunting needs. Initially, there was one gun and it was used for all hunting. The use of one all-purpose gun proved to be inadequate because deer slugs destroyed my first pump shotgun. This one horrifying experience of an inoperable gun at the age of twelve has been justification for the purchases of the exact firearm I needed for the hunt. At the age of twelve, I needed a rabbit gun and a deer gun to prevent any such future loss that could be caused by the use of an all-purpose gun.

While trying to figure out how to earn enough money to own two shotguns, I discovered that I had a need for a 22 rifle. Sometimes, just realizing a need causes something good to happen. I can't explain it, but it happens. A 22 bolt action rifle somehow came into my possession through some type of deal that I don't recall. I was happy with that rifle and it worked fine until I realized that I needed to replace the bolt action with a semi-automatic. It turned out that the bolt action was too slow to get off the number of shots that I usually needed to get a moving squirrel. The semi-automatic that I needed for squirrel hunting was obtained within a few years, and I was again a happy and properly equipped hunter. To prove that I don't get rid of a good piece of equipment, I still have that rifle and use it for an occasional squirrel hunt.

Shotguns came and went for several years. Seems a lot of guns had crooked barrels. I did finally get a fantastic pump shotgun. It was a Remington 870 Wingmaster. Dad adjusted the stock to make it fit me, and rabbits began to fear the days I went into the field. This particular gun stayed around until we started reloading shells. The heavy loads blew the ejector out of the bolt, so I decided to make a trade. I obtained my first semi-automatic.

Some people today think of them as assault weapons, but back then only rabbits and ducks saw it that way. Well, those powerful reloads continued to be a problem, and one trade later I went for a double barrel that could take the duck hunting loads that we produced.

I stopped trading shotguns. For many years, I only considered which gun I would retire, and then go buy its replacement. Of course it takes a long time to decide what to get. I made a couple of exceptions to the restriction on trading or selling of my old equipment. I made the mistake of momentarily thinking that it was okay to sell something I had retired and no longer saw a need to keep.

I acquired the gun at a fairly young age. While I was in college I bought a brand new Remington 870 Wingmaster to replace the one I traded years earlier. Soon afterward, I bought a second barrel for it. It proved to be the best shooting gun I ever owned. My trusty old pump went rabbit, quail, duck, and deer hunting. I even used it to shoot trap. I finally came to realize that I was over using my favorite gun, so I bought a deer slug gun. It was the same model as my trusty all-around gun, but with a special deer slug barrel. I mounted a scope on it and used it for deer hunting until I sold the farm. I may have forgotten to mention buying a farm so that I had a place to hunt, but that really does not fit into the category of equipment. That was an investment. Once I sold the farm, deer hunting needs changed.

Over the years a few additions were made to my collection. My trusty old Remington was seldom used and in a weak moment I offered to sell it to a friend. Then I traded the deer gun for a high end auto-loader that I use for upland game. I really should have retired those pump shotguns.

My Remington model 700 rifle in .270 caliber was bought in 1972 for deer hunting in Oklahoma. I was stationed in Oklahoma for a few months while I was in the Air Force, and I thought that I would deer hunt there. The Air Force had other ideas and I had to wait 10 years to hunt in a state that allows the use of rifles. I held onto that rifle until I finally moved to a state where rifle hunting deer was allowed. I doubted that I would ever consider retiring that rifle for anything else — it was just too good of a hunting rifle. Then because of changes in hunting opportunities, the unimaginable happened. I sold that rifle to a friend. Another mistake.

After a few years, I decided that I needed a new rifle for just in case I got a chance to go deer hunting in a state that permits rifles. I realized that my momentary weaknesses had not really changed the fact that a hunter needs to be prepared for the opportunities that may come, no matter how unlikely it is that opportunity may come. Deer hunting has changed a lot in my lifetime and those changes greatly limit the opportunities for an outdoorsman from the past. Today, you either own a farm, pay huge fees to hunt on someone else's farm, or hunt a public area along with five guys about thirty yards away. Those three options don't appeal to me, but I am an optimist. I expect to find a place where I can safely hunt without paying an outrageous fee, and I am prepared. The new rifle is a beauty.

Handguns have always held a special place in my heart — ever since I saw Matt Dillon take down the bandits on *Gunsmoke*. The first two handguns that I owned were rejects. My neighbor Bob Childers sold me the first one. Bob is the man that sold me that beautiful Stevens 16 gauge, my first ever shotgun. The handgun that he sold me was a single action 22 revolver. I used it for a few months and realized it was not something I wanted to put into a lifetime collection. I let it go in one of my later trades. My first really good handgun was a 22 High Standard Trophy model that I bought to shoot on a handgun league. Once the factory repaired it to prevent it from going fully automatic, it was really nice.

Here in the great state where I live, it is permissible to hunt deer with handguns. After two of my friends spent three years telling me about their attempts to get a deer with their handguns, I decided to get in on the action. Friendly competition is something I write about in another story. To get in on the action, I added a .357 magnum revolver to my list of needed equipment and managed to close in on one that seemed to have my name on it.

I considered trading my target pistol for a .357 magnum, but decided that considering the trade was enough. The new gun would be purchased under the new hunting adventures policy. This basically says that if hunting interests have expanded, new equipment can be purchased. I ended up going for a Smith & Wesson model 686 that proved to be a really nice gun.

Getting a new caliber of handgun creates a need for new reloading equipment. The reloader that was part of the package deal was fun to use too. I reloaded every bullet that ever went through my revolver. Not one factory load ever went in the cylinder. That was only possible because I planned ahead and bought the reloader with the gun. Planning ahead is good.

Taking two guns in the field for deer hunting may sound like too much. However, I assure you that it provides for increased flexibility. The rifle is for long shots — the handgun for short ones. The medium range shots can result in a little confusion, and I never figured out what type gun to purchase for the medium range challenges, so I decided to just default to the rifle for anything that wasn't obviously in handgun range.

I was thrilled to take one shot with my handgun and get a good size deer. Of course, I notified my friends of my success at the first opportunity. The informal rules of hunting competition required that I inform them of my success at the earliest possible time or they could accuse me of memory "improvement". They both said they were happy for me. That is required of fellow sportsmen. When only one has come out successful, the others are to be happy for their friend. One of them sold his 44 magnum hunting pistol shortly after that. I guess he didn't see any reason to compete against his other buddy for second place.

Getting agreement at home to buy the needed equipment sometimes requires a phantom trade. A phantom trade is where an existing gun is considered for trade, but then a cash deal is made at the last minute. The story told at home is usually that the gun trader was trying to get my gun for too little, and that I will just sell it to someone. Strange how that has worked out. Apparently I have acquired some very special firearms that are worth more to me than to anyone else. Nobody ever wants to pay what I think my guns are worth.

As can be seen, I kept things pretty simple for as long as I could. My needs became a little more complicated for a time, but I have again simplified. To some, I probably appear to have too much for the things I do today; to others I probably appear to come up short. But for me I have enough to hunt what I want to hunt. I think I have finally reached the point where I know when enough is enough. But then, a new catalog is expected to arrive this week.

Fishing The Snake River

TROUT FISHING

Three fishermen living in the Midwest caught every kind of fish that was native to that region, and it was time to apply their skills and perhaps expand them for trout fishing. The three fishermen were my father, my brother, and me. To expand our list of fishing successes to include trout, we had to use our vacation time for a trout fishing trip to the western mountains. We selected the small town of Pinedale, Wyoming as our destination. We didn't actually plan to fish in Pinedale. The town was our planned base for daily excursions during a ten-day trout fishing trip.

We planned our trip well in advance of leaving our hometown of Muckville. The state of Wyoming sent brochures upon my father's request, and we selected the Rivera Lodge for our stay.

Now, don't jump to any conclusions about what a lodge in Pinedale might be, because it is not the same as the massive Yellowstone Lodge near Old Faithful. It is somewhat smaller than the Yellowstone Lodge.

Regardless of its smaller size, the Rivera was perfect for our trip. This particular lodge was made up of several "cabins" that were hooked together side by side. Actually, there was no space between most of the cabins. Back at that time, similar places where adjacent cabins were hooked together were called motels.

This one was a little different and much better than a motel, because each unit actually gave the visual impression of being a cabin. It was nice. The outside was made of stained logs and the interior was exceptionally well maintained. After my years of camping in tents and camping trailers, this was plush.

Our selected lodge was located on the bank of Pine Creek, a mountain stream that ran through town. Mrs. Doris Buzzlander, the lady that operated the place was real nice. She and her husband "Buzz" started the lodge fifteen years or so before we showed up, and they knew how to treat their guests. She turned out to be the best trout fishing guide that we met on our trip.

In my sixteen years of life leading up to this trip, I used my cane pole, a trotline, or my casting rod and reel to catch every kind of fish I wanted to catch. My equipment was quite adequate for catching bluegill, catfish, bass, and an occasional crappie. Grinnell, white perch, carp, and buffalo don't count as fish because we didn't normally eat them, but I could still catch them with my trusty fishing equipment. Come to think of it, I even caught skip-jack mackerel in the Ohio River using what I owned.

Our trip to Wyoming was a special event because it would be our first serious attempt to catch trout, mountain stream trout to be specific, rainbow trout by name. My father and brother briefly tried to catch trout on a previous trip through Michigan and into Canada, but that was when I was very small and not really a fishing trip. I didn't consider that a real attempt to catch trout. So, this would be our first real attempt at getting into trout fishing in a serious way. To do this correctly, some special trout fishing equipment was needed. A cane pole wouldn't do the trick.

I religiously read sporting magazines when I was a boy. Those magazines are probably the primary reason I could read when I completed the sixth grade. It was from those magazines that I learned about the equipment needed to trout fish. Serious trout fishermen use fly rods. I would need one of those. And waders would be necessary to get to the perfect spot in a trout stream. Tennis shoes and short pants wouldn't do for the mountain streams. They worked well in lakes and ponds of the Midwest, but the water in a mountain stream was going to be a little colder.

Selecting the correct fly rod and reel was done in a scientific manner. I knew enough from my magazine reading to go on a quest to obtain exactly what I needed. I went to Peak's Sporting Goods store. It was there that I bought the best fiberglass rod and automatic reel I could get with the money I had. Mr. Peak was a big help. He had a way of guiding me to the best item I could purchase with the amount of money in my pocket.

Our fishing equipment was carefully packed in rod tubes and tackle boxes. The camp stove was packed along with our special fish frying iron skillet. Waders were carefully bundled to prevent any damage to them. We also packed a few clothes in case we decided to change before we returned home. Mom was going with us, and the clothing bags were repacked for some reason. We were ready for the day of departure to arrive.

We planned to leave on vacation at 4:00 p.m. on the last working day before vacation began. The day finally came. Everything was ready and stacked by the back door before noon, so I took the family car for a brief visit with some friends. I had a new driver's license, and going to see friends was one of the new freedoms that comes with a driver's license. Besides, I needed to remind them one last time that I would be gone for a few days on a fishing expedition to Wyoming. Mom was okay with me taking the car as long as I remembered to pick Dad up from work. No problem.

I was off to the other side of town. Our visit was great. We went into the "we're alone in the world" mode, and that has some unwelcome effects when there is any need to remain connected to reality. Time slipped past without the slightest attention paid to it. Upon realizing it was approaching 4:30 p.m., and that I was half an hour late to pick up my father from work, I bolted toward home. I shot past where Dad worked, and he wasn't there. Maybe he grabbed a ride from someone. It wasn't far to home and I arrived there a couple of minutes later. Everyone was waiting.

There were some harsh words aimed my way for delaying our departure. I was heartsick because this was the trip that I was so much anticipating. After a few minutes, everyone faced up to the fact that the clock could not be turned backward, and we put our stuff in the car and headed west. Graciously, nobody, not even my brother, ever again mentioned the late start.

We had three drivers in the family including me, and we had decided in advance that we would drive all night and then keep going the next day if not too tired. It was about 1345 miles and our estimated driving time was 19 hours and 38 minutes. We sometimes drove a little fast, and that was expected to make up for some of the time lost stopping to buy gas and to eat.

Actual travel time turned out to be almost 22 hours, so we pulled into the lodge at Pinedale during mid-afternoon, around 2:30 p.m. The excitement about being at our destination was more than I could stand, and I was ready to start fishing. After a brief period of encouraging my brother, and then my father, we headed up Main Street to the local sporting goods store that I saw as we passed through town. We needed a license and some local dry flies. I didn't really need to buy a license, but my fish would count against my father's limit if I didn't have a license. No sense in coming all this way and skimping to save a license fee. I planned to catch as many fish as my brother, and no shared limit was going to prevent that. It was one of the few times in life I had no trouble with the cost of a license.

With the license purchased, I began to look around the store. The longer I stood in that store, the more I realized I was going to need something more than I had brought along on the trip. The list began to grow. Special flies were already on the list, but now a special net would be helpful to keep the really big ones from getting away. Spare fly line, leader, more flies — maybe some fishing advice.

The best way to get advice about a place to fish is to pile up on the counter all the supplies you may purchase, and before handing over any money, ask the question. Where would a fellow go fish where he would need all this stuff? Directions to a special stream about forty miles up a gravel road were provided by the proprietor of that store. That is a lot of gravel road.

The next morning we were out the door well before daylight. Mom stayed at the lodge. After a forty mile ride up a gravel road, we came to a bridge across a small river, and three of us were ready to get out of the car. The stream looked perfect to the three of us.

It didn't take long until we caught a few trout. They were all keepers. The three of us were having some success, with me somehow seeming to be first to reach the holes that held fish. There were exciting times when the fish first took the fly and the fight began. Of course, it's also exciting when the trout is landed and goes on the stringer. Kids from the Midwest use stringers, not baskets. If pushed into it, was may use a net, but never a basket.

We found that trout fishing had other aspects to it that were exhilarating. While fishing that first flowing water, I learned to walk in a mountain stream wearing chest waders. It was quite a thrill for both feet to start going downstream when I hadn't moved either foot. As they bounced across the tops of rocks, it was a real neat trick to keep my balance and avoid filling my chest waders with cold water. Fortunately, my brother-in-law had taught me to waterski, so it was something akin to that except my feet were under water and skimming across rocks instead of across ripples on the water's surface. I managed to stay upright. Coordination problems of previous years perhaps had passed.

My dad only wore hip boots. He found that streams are sometimes different depths on two sides of a rock. This realization came by stepping up on a rock from one side, then stepping down on the other. Because the other side was sometimes twelve inches deeper than the near side, a clear signal was transmitted through his sensory system. There were actually two signals.

As one foot went down the far side, he could feel that it hadn't made contact when expected. That was signal number one. Before his foot ever touched bottom, an icy cold feeling spread down his leg as water filled his boot. That was signal number two. This boot filling experience was explained to my brother and me as something that should be avoided. He had given us a lesson through a negative example. This was an unusual method for him to use, but not completely foreign to us.

Fly casting is a real art. Anyone that fly fishes knows that it is an art form to be mastered. It took me a few minutes to master it. I could actually get my fly on the stream and make it float. The trout in this remote area were relatively smart, but not smart enough. They were trying to eat fake flies.

After we fished a stretch of the stream to the extent that we figured there wasn't any point in continuing, we returned to our lodge at Pinedale. We cleaned our fish, ate the supper Mom cooked for us, and planned the next day's fishing. Mom had spent that day at the lodge enjoying some rest and a little leisure time sitting out by Pine Creek.

For our next day of fishing, we selected another location that we heard about from the man at the store. It was a little further away. The road was a little rough, just as our sporting goods store adviser had warned.

In Wyoming, a road that is a little rough means that you should have a pack mule and be willing to do some walking. We didn't know that. A little rough meant something quite different to people back home. At least we knew three people from Muckville that weren't aware of this terminology difference. But we were quick learners and got our only needed lesson when we went fishing on our second day in Wyoming.

Our 1965 Chevy Impala was an all-purpose vehicle because my family only owned one car. We used it to transport girls to dances. We used it to transport buddies on hunting trips. We even used it to pull a fishing boat and a camping trailer. Going up a gravel or dirt road that is a little rough didn't sound like a problem.

With our fishing gear in the trunk, we departed from Pinedale on our way to catch some really big trout. The road became a little rough shortly after we left the paved highway. The further we went, the larger the boulders became that were in the road. The bottom of the car wasn't scraping bottom, so we continued forward. When we judged that we were about a half mile from the stream, we approached a steep downhill segment of the road. In Muckville, people would have called it a cliff.

The hill wasn't going to stop us after going that far. We had gone too far to turn around, and we were burning daylight. Dad liked to fish, and an unnecessary walk of a half mile wasn't our idea of a good time. Besides, walking would take up more of the early morning than continuing by car. The drop-off was assessed, and it was decided that the car probably would not end up hung on the edge of this gorge. The car crept forward to the edge of the drop off. All I could see was sky. Forward, forward, and over we went. In the next few seconds, my life flashed before my eyes — not to mention the number of things that flashed by the car window. The brakes on our car were in good shape, but they were of no value on the downhill segment of this particular cow path. Those few downhill seconds were all that I needed to decide to walk down the next cliff. Fortunately, there was enough space between the hill and the stream that Dad easily brought the car to a stop.

Thoughts about the trip down a Wyoming "little rough" road were quickly replaced with putting on waders, attaching flies to the leader, and finding the best places to approach the stream. We fished and fished that morning. The flies were expertly placed near rocks, over holes, and under the overhanging tree limbs just as they were the previous morning. Nothing. After several hours of fishing and not one fish, not even a strike, we realized it was time to go. We looked up at the road, and there it was, the cliff that we came down. The sky was starting to look like it would rain.

I wasn't sure that we could get the car back to the top. Dad explained that he would take a run at it, but try to only get enough momentum to ease over the edge. Too much momentum, and we may go airborne. That would not be good on a 1965 Chevy. With a long run at the hill, my father did exactly what he planned. Momentum carried us safely back up and over the edge. We all released the breath that we'd been holding, and then we agreed that there was no point in fishing a place to death, thus no point in returning to that spot.

Total exhaustion overtook me after releasing the tension of first going down the hill, then going back up it. As we ate dinner that evening, I decided that I might stay at the cabin the following morning to get some extra rest. My brother thought I had gone out of my mind and assured me that once he and Dad went fishing, I would be sorry that I stayed behind.

The next morning, they drove off without me. About ten minutes after they were gone, I wished I had gone with them. I began complaining, and it wasn't but another ten minutes until my mother had nearly gone out of her mind. She thought that I should sit at one of the picnic tables and relax. I took my fly rod with me and fished a couple of flies on the stream behind the cabin. Nothing. So, I sat at one of the picnic tables and tried to relax.

Mrs. Buzzlander, the lady that owned the lodge, walked up and she seemed able to read minds. She saw me sitting at that picnic table, and I guess that I was staring at the stream. After summing me up, she suggested that I might try fishing the stream. I explained that I figured the stream was fished to death.

Even an expert like me was unable to get a hit on my flies. I had already given it a pretty good try with two of my best flies.

She agreed that flies may not work, but I could catch plenty of fish if I just used the correct bait. Pulling out my fly collection, I asked which one was best. She grinned at me and said that I could put them away. Then she said that I should use bread.

That did it. A grown woman shouldn't tease a boy about being able to catch fish, and then make fun of him by suggesting bait such as bread, corn, or hot dogs. Only a city kid would do such a thing. My belly laugh probably told her that I was doubtful that her idea was going to be any help.

Just in case the laughter was not clear enough, I explained as nicely as I could that I knew better. She politely continued to insist. I finally decided to try the bread idea just to get her to be quiet. I gently cast the baited hook to a small pool in the stream. A monster trout rolled over and took the bread with him.

When I'm wrong, I'm wrong, and even at sixteen could admit it. I tried to act dignified and appreciative of the suggestion she had given. I think that the two back flips I did were enough to show my gratitude.

My father and brother returned shortly after I caught the sixth trout. I had them on a stringer that I didn't immediately show. Timing is everything when in competition, and the competition was about to begin. I engaged first by asking how their trip went. Sadly, they had not caught a fish. They had been skunked. In case you haven't heard the term before, skunked is a term used for when the competition gets nothing. I expressed some sympathy and was ready for the second stage of the competition.

After a few moments, I mentioned that I became bored and decided to fish the stream behind the cabin. I waited, but the expected question didn't come. Patience is important when in competition. I waited a little longer, and then my brother John broke the silence. "Did I catch anything?" Well, I didn't want to brag in light of their bad luck, but I responded. "Yes, I caught a few trout. I think there are six of them. That does not include the smaller ones that I released. I stopped fishing because my arm was getting tired, and I was at my daily limit." The puzzled look on his face was priceless. Victory! The competition was over, and then came the phase where I was recognized as the family expert.

Where were they caught?
I told you, in the stream behind the cabin.
No, exactly where?
Oh, ok let me show you.
What kind of fly did you use?
I wasn't supposed to tell them the secret bait, but I couldn't hold out any longer. Bread. Then, of all things, my honesty was questioned. Fine, use your best fly. Before long, they had bread on a hook and caught a few fish. I stuck around to give a few pointers.

The day ended with Dad frying fish and preparing a meal that is forever etched into my memory. This was probably the best meal of the trip for my mom. She had not been required to prepare anything for this one. It was without a doubt the best meal of the trip for

Fish fry on Pine Creek

me, because we were eating my trout. Even those caught by my fishing buddies seemed to be in part mine.

I still recall with positive thoughts the Rivera Lodge, the nights spent there, and the stream behind. Thirty years after that fishing trip, I made a special detour during a family vacation in 1996 and stopped there. I walked back to look at the creek and took a moment to recall that special day. Wow! Is there only one day like that in a lifetime?

That trip had more experiences than I've told in this short story, and there were many lessons learned during that week in Pinedale. One of those lessons is that not everything a sporting goods store owner tells a traveler is completely accurate. By my estimation, the advice we received was 33% correct. Only one of the three places he told us to fish actually turned out to be any good. Come to think about it, it is possible that the one place we did find fish was a mistake. The directions we received weren't all that clear, and it is entirely possible we ended up somewhere other than where he tried to send us.

Sometimes, things just have a way of turning out right. Sometimes, someone at a quaint little lodge offers a little help in making a vacation extra special.

Ole Smokey

RIDING HORSES

Horses are interesting animals for many reasons. They're big, powerful, fast, smart, and sometimes docile. They have an almost magnetic quality that draws boys and girls of all ages to them. What kid would not like to have a pony or horse?

Boys seem to be born with an instinctive ability to ride horses. I've met girls that were just at home on the back of a horse. This instinct can become so overwhelming, that young boys and girls are able to turn almost any object into a horse if a real one isn't available.

By the time I was three years old, I had the urge. My parents couldn't afford to buy a horse. Well then, I reasoned that a pony would do until I was older. No, a pony couldn't be kept in the garage or my room, and we didn't live in the country.

Where we lived on the edge of town wasn't really in the country, and my mother often explained that it was necessary to live away from town, out in the country, before you could keep a horse or a pony at your house. As far as that goes, no farm animals larger than a guinea fowl were permitted.

Because I wasn't able to convince her otherwise, not even through several months of whining, begging and complaining, I finally decided to improvise. I discovered that a smart four year old can create an alternate reality when necessary. A broomstick was the best alternative I had because a real horse was out of the question. To properly utilize a broomstick as a horse, I resorted to a new form of magic that I was learning to call upon when a critical need arose. The broomstick would be transformed into a horse through the use of an active imagination.

Once I had opted to use the broomstick, it only occasionally got used to sweep out the kitchen floor. Most of the time, a spell was cast upon it and it was being used as a horse.

These spells were easiest to cast when I had an urge to chase down a few bandits or renegade Indians that might be roaming through the neighborhood. After I strapped on a holster and six-shooter, the broom went through a metamorphosis right in front of my eyes. It turned into a magnificent horse in no more than a few seconds. It was beautiful with a reddish brown coat, a white blaze on its nose, a black mane and tail, and four white socks.

As I mounted the horse that had replaced the broom, we would take off after the renegades. Sometimes the culprits would be lurking behind every bush and tree in the neighborhood, and none of the grown people seemed the least bit aware of them. If it wasn't for me, many of our unsuspecting neighbors could have been ravaged and their homes ransacked.

Those early rides through the neighborhood taught me quite a lot about horse riding. By the time I was five, I knew not to jump a horse into or across a deep ditch unless the ditch is at least as wide as the horse is long. Narrow ditches are rough on broom handle horses and the rider.

Jumping ditches isn't much fun unless you can clear the entire width of the ditch. Bad things happen when you unsuccessfully jump your horse over a narrow and deep ditch. On a short jump, when the front legs get to the far side, the back legs are likely to still be on the starting side. That places the horseman such that his feet are in the middle of the ditch. While the tail end is still resting on the ground at the top of the ditch, the front end makes contact with the far side, and the riders feet extend downward toward the bottom of the ditch. For a split second, the rider is straddling the horse, with the two ends of the horse resting on the two sides of the ditch. If the rider's legs are not long enough for his feet to rest on the bottom of the ditch, his weight will rest on the back of the horse. The one inch width of the horse's back is suddenly supporting the weight of the rider and possibly his weight is applied at a sensitive location. This situation results in a sharp pain. With any luck at all, the damage will not be permanent and the rider will have children at some point in the future. The horse isn't usually as lucky, and its back is broken. Don't jump ditches on a broomstick horse.

Crying and yelling about a pain that nobody can see isn't much help when the broken horse is taken back home. Mothers don't like to sweep the floor with a broken horse.

A horse that was conjured up from a broom had some advantages over real horses. For one thing, they can go as fast as you need. There is no limit to their abilities. With the right attitude, a boy on an imaginary horse can outrun any renegade that may be in the neighborhood. They also don't eat much and are allowed to be kept in the house. That keeps them handy for immediate use should bandits unexpectedly attack.

My horses had character. When I rode them along at a steady pace, they bounced just enough to make me bounce up and down as we went along. All the neighbors knew I was on my horse when I went by. They could tell by that special bounce that my horses had. Trotting caused a slight and rapid bounce, loping had a higher and longer bounce, and running was smooth with long strides. It was a thing of beauty to ride such fantastic animals.

As I aged, it was necessary to release my herd of imaginary horses. It was emotionally painful to let them go. The other kids in middle school had already transitioned to an age where they could no longer see them. They looked at me in an odd way when I rode up on Chesty, Herald or Black Max.

After a few years, I got over them being gone. Eventually, I was no longer able to conjure up a horse from a broom or long stick. As a matter of fact, I don't know any adults that are able to perform the act of turning a broom into a horse. The ability must dwindle with age.

After I decided that I must refrain from riding any of my herd, another onslaught of whining, begging, and complaining was started in an effort to get a horse "for the family." It didn't work.

After a few years of walking or riding a bicycle everywhere I went, luck finally took a turn for the better. My older sister moved to a farm and bought several horses. My sister always shared her things with her two little brothers. How many kids have that kind of luck?

One of her horses was named Billy. He was a special horse. When I first laid eyes on him, I knew he was going to take me to special places. Billy was even more special than I could have ever hoped. He had been used in rodeos. The only thing that could have been better would have been to own a cavalry horse.

The former owner said Billy was good for kids. Didn't matter to me. I had been riding horses from the time I was four – had my own herd one time.

Silly niece thought she had some kind of claim on Billy. That was probably because she was my sister's daughter and her dad told her Billy was hers. I had to figure something out. Perhaps I could generate some kind of counter-claim that would work. Maybe convince her that horses weren't fun for girls. A few stories about flesh-eating horses might help. All those ideas were rejected, and then a miracle occurred. She shared Billy with her uncles.

Lucky for me, I had all those years of horse riding experience. I didn't need anyone to explain what to do. Just show me how to put on a bridle and saddle, and I was on my way. I needed help with the saddle only because my previous riding was all done bareback.

That first ride was exhilarating. Billy and I took off across the hill, down the other side, and started across the over-grown pasture. At the bottom of the hill, there was a gully. I didn't see it because of the tall grass. Billy was an observant horse, and he saw it. Because Billy could tell that I was an experienced rider, he didn't warn me of the gully. He simply jumped across.

Billy learned a lot in the rodeo. He could catapult himself through the air to make it appear as though he had been shot from a cannon. Thank goodness someone put a handle on the saddle. I grabbed it as Billy was about to shoot out from under me. My superman impression only lasted for a few seconds before Billy touched down on the far side of the ditch. I used the saddle handle to stop my forward movement. Fortunately, puberty hadn't yet caused my voice to change, so there wasn't any change in voice caused by the sudden stop on that handle.

I later found out that the proper name for the handle on the saddle is a horn. It took me some time to figure out why it was called a horn, because pushing on it didn't make a beeping sound. The horn on a saddle only causes a noise when the horse stops fast and the rider is impaled by it. That was it. The name was more like the horns on an animal than the kind on a car.

I considered myself an experienced horse jumper after my first ride on Billy. Because I didn't hit the ground, and I went higher than the horse, I considered the jump a success.

A few other horses lived with Billy. This permitted more than one person to ride and would probably reduce the amount of time spent arguing about whose turn it was.

All that was necessary for a couple of friends to go horse riding was to gather the horses from the pasture. Because Billy had been used in the rodeo, I was told that I should get Billy out of the pasture first, then use him to bring the other horses into the corral. This technique was to be used when more than one person wanted to ride horses.

Horse riding became quite an aerobic event. It consisted of three hours of chasing horses around an eighty acre pasture, thirty minutes of getting them saddled, and fifteen minutes of riding.

Initially, a small bucket of grain would get Billy's attention if it was carried out to the pasture. When he came to eat, a rope could be slipped around his neck to lead him to the corral. Billy wasn't very dumb. The bucket of grain idea worked about two times before he was onto it.

My brother-in-law thought he was a master horse trader. Only Billy was exempt from being traded. Maybe my niece did have a purpose in life. She could really pitch a fit if anyone mentioned Billy being considered for replacement.

The continual change in horse stock gave me an occasional challenge. Backlash was one of those challenges. The first time I saw him, a guy was working real hard to stay on his back. The guy climbed off and informed my brother-in-law that Backlash was broke and ready to be ridden. However, the man cautioned as he looked at me, that Backlash should only be ridden by experienced riders. I got the message. Only I should ride the horse.

One day, I was trying the bucket of grain trick on Billy, and it wasn't working. Backlash didn't yet know the trick, so he fell for it. I lead Backlash to the corral with only slight difficulty. Billy stood in the middle of the pasture with what looked like a smile on his face. The saddle and bridle went onto Backlash without too much trouble. Now that I had him saddled, I could go get another horse for my friend. Shouldn't take long.

Backlash didn't think much of the way his saddle fit. When I got on, he began some strange hunching motions that caused his feet to leave the ground. It only took me a second to jump back off to see if his saddle needed adjusted.

The second time I got on, Backlash shot down the entrance between the pasture and corral. It was a split rail fence with lots of splits and rough areas. I pulled both legs up to prevent having them sanded off on the sides of the fence.

We burst into the pasture at a speed that was adequate to win the Kentucky Derby. As we passed Billy, he still appeared to have that grin on his face.

Guiding Backlash wasn't too hard. I could keep him in the quarter-section (that's 160 acres) that I wanted to be in. After thirty minutes of interesting horsemanship, Backlash took me back to the barn. My friend was happy to see me come back, and asked where the other horses were at.

I explained that they had all taken to being exceptionally stubborn that day. Must have been the heat. No matter what I tried, Backlash and I couldn't seem to drive or lead them to the corral. Crazy horses! The day was ruined. There was no hope of getting them rounded up if I couldn't get it done.

My sister's horses weren't always as hard to catch as on that one hot day. Sometimes my sister would close the corral after the horses came up to the barn in the evening. This made catching them much easier the next morning.

She once did this for me when I was taking my cousin Claude to ride horses. Claude wasn't much of a horse rider yet. I don't know for sure if he even had the experience of riding imaginary horses. Not knowing his experience level, I thought that he should be treated special. Let him get some good experience.

The only two horses my sister was able to catch in the corral the night before were Billy and Backlash. I knew Claude hadn't ridden much, so I did the only thing a considerate cousin would do in this situation. I let Claude ride Backlash. It was only right. He needed to get all the experience possible in the shortest amount of time. I didn't explain much to Claude about the selection of horses, my past experience with them, or my reasoning for Backlash being his assigned horse.

For the best riding experience, I decided that we would go cross-country. Take the country road for a couple of miles, and then cut back through the woods. We were doing pretty well at first. Things changed. At about a mile from the barn, Backlash decided we should turn around. Claude began complaining about Backlash's tactics. Backlash had a tendency to turn and bite the leg of the rider when he didn't get his way. Because of Claude's loud complaining, I finally agreed that we should turn around.

Something more seemed to be bothering Backlash. I could tell that he and Claude were not making a good team. It was almost to the point that I would need to change horses with Claude. Either that or shoot him and Backlash to put them both out of their misery. The final straw came about the time that Backlash tried to lie down on Claude. Right there in the woods, the horse decided to lie down and roll over. I had never seen anything like it.

After the roll over event, we traded horses. Claude had taught Backlash so many bad habits by the time we changed horses, not even I could handle him. He took a notion that he was going back to the barn and he didn't want me along for the trip. He avoided the paths that had been worn by previous trail rides, and took a direct route that ignored gullies, briars, and tree limbs.

Jumping the gullies didn't bother me. Billy had taught me how to stay in the saddle during jumps. The tearing of the briars on my legs reminded me why some people wear chaps, but I was going to survive a few painful briar scrapes. I was still on horseback.

It was the tree branches that nearly did me in. Backlash must have been a good judge of height. He managed to run under several limbs that were just about shoulder height to him. He had a way of making me think he was going to pass a low limb, then suddenly lunge under it. He would duck his head, and here it came, scraping down his back. Lying back in the saddle 'till prone on the horse was the only hope of keeping the limb from knocking me off the horse. Leaning back as far as I could, the limb would rub down my stomach and chest. Quick hand action would prevent the limb from hanging up as it ran under my chin or nose. This was the most advanced riding of my life. Not even my imaginary stallions had thought of doing these things to their rider.

Claude was happier on Billy and was now quiet. Both horses and both riders made it back to the barn alive. Claude made some comments about me giving him the bad horse. I couldn't believe that a guest would say such a thing. We remain good friends today, but Claude never did go to my sister's house to ride horses again. I don't know why. He had as much experience in that one day as many people get in a year or two of riding. I guess he didn't really appreciate the favor I had done for him.

People remember things. Ten years after that memorable day with Backlash, Claude and his brothers bought a couple of horses and kept them on their mother's farm. Claude invited me over to go for a ride. He pointed out the horse I would ride. He said the horse liked to run. When we got back from our ride, Claude had a funny grin on his face.

Grade School

THE GOOD OLE DAYS

Camping, fishing, and hunting were three of the most important things in my life when I was a kid. Actually, they still rank very near the top of the list. Between the ages of nine and fourteen, school wasn't on my list of important things to do. I attended school regularly, I was in the assigned classes, and I usually did any homework I was given. But there were times when my heart just wasn't in it. I now realize that school was of great importance, but when I was in grade school and middle school, the teachers and my parents had a lot of work to do to make sure the important lessons were learned. I may have missed out on a few of them as a result of my passions for outdoor adventures. They must have gotten enough through to me, because somehow I became a school teacher and actually enjoyed teaching for a few years. But that is another story.

My lack of regard for the importance of school sometimes caused conflicting opinions between my teachers and me. Because of my occasional preoccupation with being somewhere other than in school, the teachers probably thought that I didn't have a very long attention span. It wasn't that I had a short attention span, I just couldn't keep my attention on the things they wanted me to do.

In addition to the obvious benefit of getting an education, school's next biggest and most obvious benefit to me as a boy was that it provided the time and a place to plan camping, fishing, and hunting trips. It was normally quiet at school, and interruptions to the planning process only took place occasionally. Some interruptions were caused by other kids, such as Burt. He would tend to do something disruptive when he became bored with what the teacher was doing. He had one habit in particular that almost always resulted in getting me in trouble.

Burt seemed to know just when the time was right to capture my attention and tempt me into an action that would focus our teacher's attention upon me. One method he used to get my attention was to sit perfectly still and make not one noise. He knew that by doing so he was making himself a perfect target for a spitwad. Just in case you aren't aware, back in the good ole days, a spitwad was created by putting a small piece of notepaper in my mouth and getting it wet and soft. Not sloppy wet, just soft and pliable. Then the paper was rolled between my finger and thumb to make a neat sphere. I could use my index or middle finger in the process. Either worked just fine.

Burt knew that I couldn't stand for him to sit there like a perfect target, so I'm sure he did it just to get me in trouble. Sure enough, about the time he sat still for what seemed like an eon, I fell to the temptation, and then the teacher would simultaneously get in a bad mood.

Now, there is no connection between a well-developed spitwad shot and any other form of marksmanship. But somehow, at my age back then, anything shot with accuracy was a cause for joy.

A well-aimed spitwad would hit Burt right behind an ear. He would yell as if hit with a blast from a bazooka, and then turn to blame me. Whether or not my fingers were wet, the teacher assumed that I caused Burt's sudden outburst. Not once did she ever scold Burt for failing to have the self-control required to avoid yelling when hit by an unexpected spitwad or rubber band.

Rubber band shooting was rarely done in school. For some reason, we were not allowed to have rubber bands. If at any time I had a rubber band to shoot, someone else brought it in the room and had already shot it at me. So, occasionally I would have one and would pass it along to Burt for him to keep or shoot according to his pleasure. Paper, well it was everywhere.

I suppose it was only logical for our teacher to blame me for any direct hit on Burt. It was known throughout the school that I was a superior marksman. The general knowledge regarding my ability with sporting arms was enough reason for some people to suspect that I was also deadly accurate with spitwads and rubber bands.

Nobody at school had actually seen a demonstration of my marksmanship in the field, but they had come to know of my abilities through stories I was willing to share. I found it easiest to share my stories with the rest of the class while the teacher rambled on about train speeds and distances between towns. Nobody near me, except for possibly Burt, was interested in that stuff. Sporting adventures were far more interesting. Should the teacher feel our group was spending too much time in class discussing things other than trains, she would sometimes make us spend an extra half hour together after school. This was perfect for thirty minutes of group activity focused on our favorite outdoor adventure or possibly for planning the next event.

To continue to explain about spitwad occurrences, I'll mention that my teacher seemed to be biased. I think Burt may have been her pet student. She always gave Burt the benefit of the doubt, and then she would start looking for a way to make me pay a price for what he started. A journey to the principal's office might be required if Burt had too many moments of exaggerated pain. A trip to the principal's office is dreaded by most students. I learned to use it in a positive manner. A trip to the office wasn't all that bad the way that I looked at it. At least I wouldn't be sitting in class hearing the end of the train story or trying to figure out where two trains would collide.

One problem that I had with my teachers was that they didn't teach lessons that related to anything I could use in my lifetime. Not once did they explain how to calculate the amount of main staging (string) to purchase for a trotline when a person knows the number of desired hooks to go on the trotline. My teachers insisted that I learn to calculate various things regarding train speeds and distances between towns.

I had no desire to figure out the point at which two trains would collide if they left two towns at different times going at different speeds. There wasn't any need to do that. The railroad companies had people who created schedules. Besides, I wasn't planning any train trips and the train companies were already in a downward spiral. I am an adult now and have never worked for the railroad, so I am quite happy that I didn't mess with learning about train calculations. What we should have been doing was calculating how long it would take for the train companies to go broke if they stayed on the same path.

My lack of concern regarding train calculations caused some of my teachers to form inaccurate conclusions about my attention span. My attention span was far better than they ever realized. Some days I arrived at school by 8:00 a.m., worked all day on the plans for a fishing trip, departed from school at 3:30 p.m. and prepared my equipment for the trip before 4:00 p.m. Sticking to one activity for eight hours should be proof of an adequate attention span.

Planning was occasionally interrupted by school related activities, but it didn't mean that my attention was fully diverted. The planning process was only temporarily suspended and was resumed at the first opportunity. As mentioned earlier, one type of interruption was a trip to the principal's office.

An excursion to the principal's office was usually brought on by an outburst from one of my teachers. It seemed that almost any small thing could cause my teachers to have an emotional outburst. One example was the time I brought the rattle from a snake to class and twitched it a few times while the room was real quiet.

A momentary break in my planning process was required so that I could do some quick thinking during the walk to the principal's office. It wasn't a long walk, and I needed some unique good reasons why I shouldn't be swatted by a paddle when I opened the door.

My modest success in life can be partially attributed to the school system in Muckville. Not that they had a particularly excellent curriculum or anything like that. The success I attribute to them comes more from the planning techniques developed while in school. They were valuable to me both as a teacher and as an aerospace engineer. They even come into play when writing stories.

Two types of planning techniques were learned.

The first was leisurely planning in which all the time in the world is available. This planning technique is good when preparing to do something for which you have very limited resources. As a grade school kid, I didn't have much hunting, fishing, or exploring equipment, so I had to make very carefully thought out plans.

The second type of planning requires rapid thinking and an ability to think under pressure. The trips to the principal's office taught me to plan under pressure.

I was never held back in grade school. The teachers seemed to always think it best for me to move forward. In my six years there, I noticed that grade school teachers form opinions and hold grudges. Fortunately, after six years of grade school, I graduated to junior high school. I had already completed 35 rabbit hunting trips, 60 weekend camping trips, 72 fishing trips not including the weekend camping trips, hunted in five counties, fished in 12 lakes and 2 rivers. I'll not tally the hiking trips, exploration adventures, baseball teams, swimming teams, or myriad other learning focused activities that were already logged.

Transitioning from grade school to junior high seemed like a beneficial break. It gave me a chance to start over again. Perhaps the teachers in junior high could be brought to understand the importance of camping, fishing, hunting and other activities connected with outdoor adventures.

No way! These teachers were worse than the ones in grade school. Things really had been better in grade school. Those were the good ole days.

Only one of my junior high teachers enjoyed camping, and he was a shop teacher that didn't realize the value of the knowledge I was willing to share with him. He thought he already knew everything about the outdoor world and that not even an expert such as I could provide any helpful information. Being part of my nature to be a helpful kid, I decided that I would find another way to assist Mr. Button. If he wouldn't listen to my stories about camping, perhaps I would be able to help him when it was time to demonstrate the correct use of the power tools.

Because none of the teachers seemed to be interested in hearing about my outdoor adventures, I decided to talk to Burt about them. He also made it to middle school the year that I did, and again he was in many of my classes. He seemed to have plenty of time on his hands. Besides, he thought of himself as a hunter and could most likely benefit from some of my experiences. Burt probably got the impression that he knew how to hunt because his father occasionally took him hunting. Knowing Burt, I figured that his father did all the shooting and then let Burt think he had been of help.

Burt realized that his role during our unauthorized classroom discussions was to learn from me, but a little feedback would have helped me know what to repeat and when I could move on. But there he sat, and listened, while I explained the correct way to do things. The one thing that he did to irritate me was sit there and act like he wasn't part of the conversation. He was good at that. He was so good that it would throw the teacher off his trail and cause her to pick on me. Burt wasn't being a very good friend.

The seventh grade deer season was approaching and it was going to be a special event. My dad, brother and I were lucky enough to get deer permits. Having spent a lot of time planning for an eventual deer hunt, receiving deer permits was something like winning the lottery.

I had been doing some reading on the proper ways to field dress a deer, just in case I should ever get to harvest one. I found a perfect one page article in one of the popular sporting magazines of that time. I tore the page out of the magazine and put it in my hunting coat pocket.

The details of how to field dress a deer included a thorough description of how to use the knife and how to use a piece of string, or a shoelace, during a crucial step in the process. So, I bought a new knife, got me a piece of string, and carried them both in my coat pocket along with the instructions. I was prepared.

Buying that special knife is a story all in itself. I wouldn't have known for sure that I needed a special deer cleaning knife if I hadn't wandered into Peak's Sporting Goods store one day. When he found out that I had some lawn mowing money, and was planning a deer hunt, he showed me just the kind of knife I needed. The price was just right, too. I could afford it. There was even some change left over to go by Mamie's Sweet Shop and buy a soda. That gave me a chance to let my new knife be exposed where a few people might notice it. You couldn't do that today for fear of someone thinking you are starting one of those deranged attacks. Anyway, I had a special deer cleaning knife, and I was ready to go hunting.

Burt did finally talk one day and mentioned that he and his father managed to get permits for the deer season. I couldn't help but snicker to myself a little. Not out loud because that would have been rude. I questioned Burt some, and he didn't understand why I thought that perhaps he should pass on this deer season. He really wasn't old enough to be going deer hunting. He said something about being as old as me.

Deer season was split into two three-day segments back then. Each segment opened on Friday, one in November and one in December. Because season started on Friday, my father had to take a day off work without pay for us to hunt on opening day. That was a real show of hunter dedication because his job at Mize-O-Matic hardly paid enough to live on. My brother and I also had to make a major sacrifice to get to hunt opening day. We had to take a day off from school. That too was a real show of hunter dedication. I'm not sure what my brother missed on that day away from school, but I wasn't going to be diagraming sentences in English class. Now, that was a disappointment.

Sometime before opening day, I managed to trade my single barrel shotgun for a used 20 gauge Stevens pump. It took pretty much all the lawn mowing money from the previous summer. I was the happiest boy in the state. I could now put three slugs in my shotgun and be ready for any possible situation.

The first morning of deer season, I saw a doe emerge into the corn field at about 150 yards. It turned and walked parallel to the fencerow I was in. It stayed approximately 38 yards from the fence. When it was broadside to me, I took careful aim and began to squeeze the trigger. At just the last moment, I realized that I didn't really want to shoot a doe, so I flinched to cause the slug to hit the dirt near its feet.

The well placed shot had the desired effect. It scared the doe enough that it ran full bore to the deepest section of woods. That would be a safe place to hide for the rest of the season, which was the exact effect I had wanted. Real hunters such as me would wait for a big buck.

I didn't see another deer that I felt was big enough to shoot. As a matter of fact, I didn't see any more deer that were within 200 yards. It's just as well. The used Stevens pump that I purchased turned out to be junk and a spring inside had broken on the first shot. It never was right after that. The risk associate with used gun deals is another story.

When I returned to school the Monday following the November deer season, Burt was all smiles. I didn't ask him what he was so happy about. He and I were already in the great competition of outdoor sportsmen, and I had already learned some of the rules. Waiting for me to ask, he nearly exploded. He couldn't stand it any longer, and at 10:00 a.m. he blurted out something about some small twelve point buck. I suspect that it wandered in front of his gun so close that it was dangerous to pull the trigger. Not being too bright, Burt didn't realize the danger or unsportsmanlike behavior of shooting a deer that is too close. Regardless of the danger involved, it seems that he somehow managed to get the darn thing. He talked about it so much that at 10:01 a.m. I had to ask the teacher to have him be quiet. This was a real turn of events. He was distracting me, and I couldn't hear what she was saying about the sentence diagrams.

Burt was so persistent that I couldn't believe what was taking place. He had the nerve to ask our teacher for permission to tell his story to the whole class. I was so embarrassed for him. Then of all things, she gave him permission. I couldn't believe it. All year she had been telling me to stop telling hunting stories, now she was giving Burt permission to tell one to the entire class.

I never knew a person could go on for so long about such a lucky chain of events. Burt finally finished his story. When he returned to his chair, he asked me how I had done. He might as well have shot me, but I was working on my skills for future exchanges of this type. I changed the subject by asking him a question.

When asked if he had field dressed his deer, Burt said that he hadn't. His father had done it. That was all I needed. Nobody lets someone else field dress their first deer. It's like letting someone else marry your fiancé. It just isn't done.

A beginning story teller might occasionally slip up and tell something that others will point out as a weakness in the story. Such was the case with Burt. The weakness in his story was the fact that his father field dressed the deer. Everyone in our seventh grade English class still wonders why Burt didn't field dress that deer.

As a seventh grader, I had a tendency to listen very carefully to adults telling hunting and fishing stories so that I might learn from their story telling techniques. Having already been involved in several challenges to my stories, I thought I should learn all that I could.

I learned that it isn't a real good idea to point out the weaknesses in another person's story. It just isn't good story telling etiquette, and could cause others to start questioning every story they hear. However, proper story telling etiquette does permit a challenge under certain circumstances. If a person is about to ask, or has asked, an unwelcome question, it is all right to point out something that brings suspicion on that person's favorite story. As an example, I never did answer the question about how well I had done on my first deer hunting trip, but somehow he would end up explaining again why he hadn't field dressed his first deer. He seemed to not mind too much and it was better to hear his story than to attempt telling mine.

Junior high school was sometimes okay, but then there were times when I thought some improvement would be possible. It seemed that I was in a school full of teachers who were uninterested in my outdoor adventures. The lack of understanding in grade school combined with the lack of junior high school teachers interested in the outdoors had caused me to develop deep feelings of disappointment about school. Thank goodness junior high school only lasted two years. High school would be better.

High school was far better than grade school or junior high. We got out at 3:15 p.m. Getting out of school that early was great. I could walk home and slip on my hunting clothes and go hunting for an hour before it got dark. My friend Happy and my dogs Chester and Herman were always ready to go as soon as I could get out the door. Happy didn't know a lot about hunting, but he was willing to listen to me. It wasn't too long before he had perfected many of the hunting techniques that I demonstrated for him.

Teachers in the ninth and tenth grade had it made during rabbit season. There was no way that I was going to do anything to upset them. If I messed up and got a detention during rabbit season, the town would have to bury Happy, Chester, Herman, and me. The evening hunt gave all of us something to live for.

The rabbits along Pond Creek weren't too thrilled about our daily hunting trips. It wasn't that we were shooting many of them, but we were impacting their daily schedules. It only took a few days for them to catch on and go into hiding before we would show up. Even Herman and Chester couldn't find them. It seems that every rabbit along Pond Creek went into hiding at 3:15 p.m. Having trained all the rabbits along a two mile stretch of the creek, Happy and I decided to discontinue our evening rabbit hunts at the end of my tenth grade rabbit season.

Eleventh grade teachers didn't get as good a break as those in the ninth and tenth grade. Staying after school for an hour was no big deal, because during the eleventh grade I was doing my hunting before school. This was possible because I had switched my weekday hunting interests from rabbits to ducks.

My buddy Tripper and I decided to build a duck blind on the Muckville city lake. Actually, we adopted and fixed up a duck blind that was abandoned by older hunters. We impressed a lot of other old pro duck hunters with our abilities that year. The first impression we made was with our camouflage job on the blind. There weren't many trees left around our neck of the lake, and it appeared that we were hunting out of a huge low lying tree.

I was our expert decoy setter and duck caller. After all, I had bought the twelve decoys and the duck call. A friend of my brother had a duck calling record that I borrowed to learn duck calling. Two days of practice and my mother told me that I was sounding pretty good and wouldn't ever need to practice again. In fact, she told me that too much practicing can actually have some negative effects on a duck hunter's health. I was ready.

School morning duck hunting trips were eventually terminated. There was something about them that bothered my early morning teachers. Completely different concerns were voiced by the afternoon teachers. The two things combined were too much to overcome.

I still think they should have left well-enough alone. There weren't a lot of ducks being harvested while we were on the lake. That was good for the duck population, and it prolonged the day of hunting for the other hunters that didn't need to leave for school.

Tripper and I could only get to hunt for a few minutes each morning. We would arrive before daybreak, and then if we were lucky we would see a couple of ducks, then we hiked back to the car, drove home, and got to school before the tardy bell. If we stretched the hunting time, it was a mad dash back to the car and a quick drive into town.

An attempt was made at home to wash off the face-black. Most of it came off on the towel if we scrubbed hard enough while drying. Sometimes, a few smudges would remain on our faces. A change of clothing was necessary because the school frowned on hunting clothes in the classroom. Not too much of the smelly blue mud would get transferred to our school clothes as we changed.

Best I can remember, the complaint of our first hour teachers was that the mud was too smelly and the face-black made us look nasty. I still don't see why it bothered them. They should have been accustomed to a smudged face and an unusual odor. The Beetle twins always looked nasty and smelled funny.

The morning teachers never did see the advantages they were getting from my duck hunting efforts. The way I saw it, at least two of the students in their classes were wide awake and had interesting stories to share with the rest of the class. If we had not gone hunting, everyone in class would have still been half asleep, and nobody would have had anything interesting to tell.

Our afternoon teachers complained about the fact that duck hunters need a mid-afternoon nap. Anyone that gets up at 4:00 a.m. to do something of interest deserves a chance to catch up on their sleep, and teachers should realize this.

It is amazing how much effort a boy must go through to raise the awareness of his teachers regarding things that interest a boy that loves the outdoors. I'm glad that my teachers tolerated my adventurous nature and managed to give me what turned out to be a fairly good education. I'm also glad that I took the time to help my teachers understand what made me tick. It probably made life easier for the next kid that came along.

Boy, those were the good ole days.

The Fence

CROSSING FENCES

Crossing Fences is something that every hunter must be able to do. There may be a place where a person can hunt and not encounter a fence, but that is not the case in the Midwest. To the casual observer, there isn't anything special about crossing a fence. Just climb up one side and down the other. But then, going over is not the only way to cross a fence. There are other ways to get to the other side.

During my adult life, most of my successful fence crossings were accomplished by going over the top. The proper technique was learned from my father, but then I didn't realize he had taught me the proper and best technique until I tried a few others.

My first hunting trip took place when I was eight years old. Sure enough, on the very first trip I needed to get to the far side of a fence. Dad walked to a fence post, put his weight on the post, and went over while ever so lightly putting his boot on the barbed wire. It was almost like a ballet move. His weight went onto his hand atop that wooden post, he levitated upward and rotated while his feet appeared to ever so lightly touch the wires. I had seen him do it, but there was no way in the world I was going to suspend myself over barbed wire. Not on one hand. I was eight years old, and I had plans to live a full and complete life without barbed wire scars.

Dad was trying to convince me to cross when our dog Daisy walked up. She gave me a rather strange look, then showed me an alternative for getting to the other side. She simply ducked her head, crouched down, and walked under the fence. Because the bottom strand of wire was about fifteen inches from the ground, she cleared the fence with no trouble at all.

One demonstration from her was all that I needed. Going under the fence looked far easier than going over the top. Trouble was, I was more than fifteen inches tall. Even on all fours, I would go a little more than fifteen inches. At eight years old, it wasn't like me to give up on a good idea very easily.

Already being a keen observer of wildlife activity, I was able to put to use the abilities I had noticed a snake using to its advantage. I dropped to my belly and made a couple of slithering moves and slid under the fence. My slithering being much like that of a snake, I was able to move rather well. The mud under the fence helped to make my first efforts at slithering a little easier.

Once to the other side, Dad handed me my gun. He was now looking at me with the same level of disbelief that was on Daisy's face a few minutes earlier. He mumbled something about trying to get the mud off me before we got home.

Barbed wire fences didn't give me much trouble that year. Going under them became something of an art. I got a great deal of pride out of going under a fence faster than my dad could get over one.

My brother was a couple of years older than me, and about twice as big. He liked my method of going under a fence, but it didn't work very well for him. The art of slithering requires that your rear half be kept very low. Failing to do this can result in something getting caught by a barb on the fence.

It gave me great pleasure to slither under a fence faster than my brother could climb across the top. It also caused him some level of irritation. Safely getting to the other side of a fence before the other one was part of our competitive hunting system. Whoever got through the fence first had an advantage for getting to the ideal spot to stand while Daisy circled a rabbit.

John couldn't stand being beaten at anything, so he started a search for a faster method of crossing fences. He did discover a quick way to get to the other side. It came to him during a situation that was something of an emergency. There is nothing like a perceived emergency to bring about some quick actions that may or may not involve a lot of deep thought. We were hunting on a relative's farm in Johnson County and were walking across his pasture when the bull decided to come check us out. We weren't real sure of the bull's intentions, so we made a hasty retreat toward the edge of the pasture. Once there, I did a belly flop and slithered under the fence.

Safely on the other side, I pulled myself to my feet. As I got up, I was thinking the bull must have surely gotten my brother because he couldn't cross a fence as fast as I could slide under it. But there he was — waiting for me. Not enough time had passed for him to climb the fence and cross it in the usual manner. No way, he couldn't move that fast. Then I saw them — long scratch marks in his clothing that ran the full length of his body. They were spaced about six inches apart.

As he turned, I saw that he had a similar set of scratches down his back side. That was when I realized John had found another way to get on the far side of a fence — go through the middle. It made sense. He was on a diving team back in Muckville, and diving was second nature to him. At the speed we were running, instinct took over and he just dove right between strand numbers two and three on that fence. The spacing of the strands was a little bit close and that is why he had those scratches down the lengths of his clothes. Luckily none of the barbs caught hold and put stripes down his body.

I probably don't need to tell anyone that I don't recommend going through the middle of a fence while at full speed. Any miscalculation on your trajectory could result in those clothes scratches going a little deeper on one side than the other. Only with a bull closing in behind you would such a move be justified, and then it may be better to face the bull.

A slow motion study of a person going through the middle of a barbed wire fence isn't a pretty thing, but it does show an alternative to climbing a fence. The process can actually be used without injury if an appropriate amount of care is taken. In fact, we worked on improving the process for those times when we approached a fence at slow speed.

The process works best on an old fence that has the posts separated by twenty feet or more. Half way between the posts, the lower strand of wire can be pressed down to provide clearance for your body to pass through. Of course, the strand should never be pressed down enough to stretch the wire. Farmers don't like to have their fences sag after you have crossed them. If a buddy that you trust is nearby, it's a good idea to have him lift on strand two, thus creating an even wider gap to pass through.

My experience going through fences had limited success. The usual predicament that results from an attempt to go through is that I get stuck somewhere near halfway. One arm, my head and neck, and one leg usually make it to the far side, then a barb catches on the back of my coat or on the back of the second leg. Animation is suspended at that point until someone gets me unstuck, or I decide to rip some clothing. It's embarrassing to come home with my clothes in tatters.

Barbed wire fences in the Midwest seem to be built to cause the wire strands to spin around the moment something is on a barb. When the wire strand spins around, whatever is caught on the barb gets wound around the wire and can never be released. This is to make sure that anything touching a barb is permanently caught.

I quit replacing hunting clothes that I catch on barbed wire fences, and my hunting coat is now a coat of many colors from all the patches. To prevent completely ruining my clothes, I recently decided to stop going through fences. From now on, I will either go over or under the fence. Going through the middle is reserved for emergency crossings only.

Barbed wire fences aren't the only kind of fence that can cause a problem. Hog wire provides its own special set of challenges. Especially bad are those with one or two rows of barbed wire at the top of the hog wire. The rectangular shapes in the welded wire mesh of a hog fence are made to look like a foot hole. Just about the right size to insert a size eleven rubber boot.

Now, the correct way to cross a fence is to lean on the fence post and put as little weight as possible on the fencing material. That takes us back to the beginning of this story where my father demonstrated getting across a fence. Putting weight on the fencepost prevents stretching the wire and is greatly appreciated by the farmers. But try as hard as I can, sometimes things don't work out. Sometimes, I'll end up perched midway across the fence with all my weight on the old fence post. At about this time, a slight slip puts a splinter about an inch long into my hand. Trying to relieve the pain, I release my grip on the post and transfer my weight to one foot. At that moment the rectangular shape of the hole in the fence is reformed to the exact shape of my boot. My boot is now firmly attached to the fence, and my foot is in it.

The best way out of this mess is to remove the boot and climb down from the fence. After performing surgery with my hunting knife to remove the splinter that started the trouble to begin with, a few minutes can be spent extracting the boot from the fence. A little extra time is spent reforming the fence to keep the farmer from being upset.

Once the hand is bandaged and the fence mended, it is time to put the boot back on and return to hunting. The smell of the mud on this side of the fence reminds me of why the hog fence was used instead of barbed wire. My wife was not happy about washing that sock.

It would be a major oversight if I were to forget to mention a special kind of fence. When I was perhaps ten years old and still learning about fences, my dad showed me what an electric fence looks like. He warned of how much some electric fences hurt, and suggested that I try to avoid getting any firsthand experience. This was another of the lessons in life that I listened to, and I did my best to avoid any smooth strand of wire that was mounted on electrical insulators.

Many of my young companions also learned about electric fences. Some learned by word of mouth, others learned the hard way. Any new electric fence that went up around a cow pasture near Muckville provided at least one lesson before word got out to the boys.

One of my buddies that had never heard of an electric fence found out about them one day when he had to relieve himself. It was a long way back to the Muckville City Park and its public facilities, so he decided that he would just stand behind a tree and take care of business. Well, there was an electrical insulator on the side of that tree, and a smooth wire was tied to it. I didn't see exactly what happened because my buddy had been given an appropriate amount of privacy, but the yelling made it obvious that the fence was properly working.

When I was still in high school, my father and I had a favorite squirrel hunting place along the Big Muddy River bottoms. Today, that place is in the middle of Rend Lake. Back when we hunted squirrels there, it was in the middle of nowhere. Dad would park the car at the side of a country road, and we walked across fields for about ten minutes to get to the area of woods that we hunted. The first quarter mile required that we go along the edge of a soybean field. On most mornings, the dew would be so heavy that the tall soybeans would get us good and wet by the time we arrived at the first fence.

The fence was an old hog wire fence that was in poor condition. Because the field was being used for cattle, there was a smooth wire mounted on insulators on the pasture side of the posts. Because we were usually wet by the time we got to this point, a great deal of care was taken in avoiding contact with that smooth wire. We never did test the wire to see if it was hot, we just assumed it was.

The clouds began to build during one morning of hunting, and a rainstorm moved in. I moved under a leaning tree near one of my favorite hickory trees hoping to stay dry and continue hunting. It was raining so hard that my tree was not keeping me very dry. Dad found me there and suggested that we head for the car. Within about five steps, my clothes were soaking wet. We walked out of the woods and crossed the pasture. As we approached the fence, I was looking at it and somewhat focused on the smooth wire. Dad suggested that we be extra careful with the electric fence because were both soaked to the bone, and with the cattle in the pasture, the fence was sure to be turned on. Careful sounded good to me. Not sure why Dad thought I needed to be told to be careful.

Before he started across, Dad gave me some last minute instructions. I was to use the butt end of my gun to hold the electric fence out of his way while he crossed it. This would probably work because I had been vigilant to keep my gun as dry as possible. After Dad was over, he would hold the electric wire out of my way. He only made one mistake. He used the 'D' word. He said, "Whatever you do, don't let that wire slip off the butt plate."

Not wanting to fail my dad, I held the wire way down low to keep it out of his way. Several seconds went by, and the wire wasn't moving, but it was as tight as a fiddle string. Dad waited long enough to make sure I had it in a secure position, then he began to climb. Each movement he made caused my nerves to become tenser. The tension was working on my nerves in a way that I could not control, and my muscles began to twitch ever so slightly. It doesn't take a lot of twitching for a smooth wire to start moving on the butt plate of a shotgun. The wire began moving, and my ever so slight adjustment of the pressure didn't help. When the wire slipped from the butt plate, the tension on the wire caused it to spring upward at a high rate of speed. It was like the fully drawn string on a bow being released.

I saw it. My father saw it. It was as though time stood still for everything except that wire. Neither of us could move. Even the wire moved in slow motion sort of like one of those scenes in a movie where you know what is going to happen, but nobody can do anything to stop it.

Dad was poised in a position that had one leg across the fence. The second leg was being raised slightly, but he was still straddling 'the wire'. He was only a moment away from safety, but the second leg could not move in the available time. I hoped the wire might catch on his shoe, or the calf of his leg, perhaps even his thigh. But it didn't. The wire travelled all the way to the most undesirable location I can imagine.

Once the wire made contact, the slow motion experience was over. Dad's next move was the fastest one I ever saw him make. In reality, I didn't actually see it. After the wire made contact, there was just a blur. Then Dad was standing on the other side of the fence. Something told me to avoid eye contact.

There was a roaring noise that at first sounded like a clap of thunder rolling in from a distant lightning strike. Then I realized it was Dad yelling something. He didn't normally yell at me except when I messed up real bad, and he apparently thought this was one of those special occasions.

I'm not sure just what he was saying. If I did hear it, I probably couldn't write it here. Not that Dad had a foul mouth. He didn't. But this was one of those times when anything may have been said. I think the electric shock must have momentarily affected his speech pattern or something. Moments later when he had calmed down, he pointed at his gun that I had been holding and asked that I hand it to him. Now what was I to do? I wasn't sure that I wanted to give him his gun just yet.

I decided to stall and ask a few questions about his condition and attitude. All I asked was whether or not the fence was actually turned on. His answer wasn't real complex. It was the way he said it that told me I had asked enough questions. Simply put, his response was, "What do you think?" While pondering his answer, I realized that I had a problem. Regardless of whether I kept the guns or not, I still had to cross the fence. I handed over the guns and hoped for the best.

On Trail

GOOD BEAGLES

My childhood and early adult life were blessed with some of the best rabbit dogs in the country. There was Daisy, Chester, Herman, Snoopy, and Ernie. All the dogs we owned early in my life, and one that we borrowed, were great. I'll explain about barrowing beagles later.

That run of good, or great, beagles lasted until I turned thirty. I don't know what happened then, but things really changed. Perhaps the gene pool for beagles was contaminated in some manner or another.

The first beagle I ever hunted over was Daisy, and it turned out that she was also the best beagle. That statement may hold true for the rest of my life. It's not that I have given up on ever seeing an equally good, or better, beagle. It's just that the last dogs I owned may have been brain damaged, and I may now be too old to train more dogs. I'll also say now, that I cared deeply for those last dogs, even if there cranial contents were suspect.

When I owned those last two beagles, people sometimes suggested that I replace them, but they didn't understand that when my family gets a dog, it becomes a part of the family. Just because a member of my family is "challenged" in some manner is no reason to get rid of him.

Yes, Daisy was something special. She had a sense that told her where rabbits were located. She might be walking down a plowed field when her senses would take over. She'd stop, take a long look at a patch in a thicket, maybe twitch her nose a couple of times to see if any molecules of rabbit scent were in the air. If her muscles tensed up ever so slightly, there was a rabbit about to have a beagle on its trail. More often than not, if she tensed up, there was going to be rabbit for supper.

The last dogs I had would also walk down plowed fields, but it wasn't the same as when Daisy did it. These crazy animals walked the field because they didn't like to have the briars catch on them. Only time they seemed to tense up was when I yelled at them to get in the thickets.

I was very young when I first started hunting over Daisy. Observing my dad during those early hunts, I could tell he was completely satisfied with her performance. It was a look that I practiced, hoping to get to use it when I had beagles of my own. I got to use that look a few times when I had Ernie, but the need for it seldom came up while I had Ben and Critter. But they had some good days too.

Observing my dad wearing the look of satisfaction one day, I commented that Daisy must be about the best beagle that ever lived. His look improved a little, but he told me a story about another dog. Dad's stories were short and to the point.

"Daisy's pretty good, but you should have seen her mom. Lady was the best dog that I ever saw." That statement was a story in itself. It told me that Lady was an amazing animal. If my dad said she was better than Daisy, she definitely had made an impression on him.

There is no doubt that Lady was the greatest beagle ever. I never saw her, but because my dad said that Lady was better than Daisy, she had to be the best, because I am certain that I never saw a beagle that was better than Daisy.

A good friend is the best way to get a good beagle. Buying them doesn't seem to work. Nobody sells a good beagle. Not even the dog trainers. When was the last time anyone saw a dog trainer that didn't have good beagles to demonstrate. It's hard to impress people with your training ability if you sell your best beagles.

Lady belonged to my dad's best friend, and they hunted together a lot of the time. Having noticed my dad gleaming over her every time they went hunting, his friend decided to give him one of Lady's pups. That pup was Daisy.

Daisy was our family pet, and the best hunting dog anyone could ever want. Even my late cousin who owned dogs that competed in field trials remembered Daisy as the best he ever saw. Of course, my cousin never saw Lady. But his complement regarding Daisy was pretty amazing considering that his dogs had won field trial events.

Daisy aged and we obtained a couple of pups for our future hunting. They were named Chester and Herman. Chester was the most hardheaded dog that ever lived, but he hunted hard and would do a pretty good job of running a rabbit. My brother's friend Terry Collins gave me Herman when he was a puppy. Herman was backup to Chester. He seemed happy there, and sometimes would get to take the lead if Chester missed a turn in the trail.

Snoopy had capabilities that placed him somewhere between Daisy and Chester. He belonged to Francis Claunch, a neighbor of my sister. Francis did not hunt, but his beagle loved to run rabbits. So, Francis let us take Snoopy hunting. Snoopy was among the best when it comes to trailing rabbits. His one bad habit was that he would also run a deer trail if he came across one. He lost a few points for doing that.

Having been blessed by hunting over a dog like Daisy, I developed rather high expectations for beagles. Would I ever be satisfied with another beagle? I got lucky on the first beagle that I owned after growing up. His name was Ernie. Ernie was also a family pet, and a fine dog. Not as good as Daisy, but still a fine dog. Ernie has his own special story that needs to be told. He and I were buddies, and we had some special hunts together.

A good beagle deserves to get to hunt as much as possible, and so does a good hunter. As the hunter, I went through a period of several years when I was not able to go rabbit hunting. About a year into that period, I decided that something had to be done to let Ernie the beagle hunt. It was one of the hardest decisions of my life. I gave Ernie to a farmer that enjoyed hunting. It was my intention to spare Ernie of the torture I was going through.

As I said, I gave Ernie to the farmer. Ernie was not sold. A dog as good as that one doesn't get sold. Nobody has enough money to pay what they are worth. Besides, a member of the family isn't supposed to be sold. They are allowed to grow up and they often leave to pursue happiness, but they are never sold.

The years when I was unable to hunt caused more anxiety than I could stand. It became imperative that I find a way to return to rabbit hunting. Getting back into rabbit hunting was something like getting to breathe air again after diving too deep while snorkeling.

It is a great feeling to return to something that sustains life. Getting to restart an activity where there is such a passion, there can be a tendency to start too quickly. You could find yourself jumping into something a little early, or settling for something that is not what it is thought to be. I'll use the analogy of our need for breathing. When snorkeling, a person that goes too deep for too long may upon resurfacing try to take a breath of air a little too soon and choke on water.

When I was returning to the sport of rabbit hunting, there was a tendency to try to start too quickly. One problem with anyone attempting a rapid return to rabbit hunting is that a person may end up taking the first dogs available.

Having snorkeled some, I understood about being cautious when in a hurry. I decided to try and take the needed time to find the right dogs, rather than jump into something and get a couple of rejects. I called a beagle club to see if they could direct me to a good place to get some beagles, but they weren't much help because I wasn't a member of their group. They offered to sell me a couple of runts, but I decided to pass.

It so happened that my mother knew that an uncle of one of my cousins had started raising beagles. What luck, a sort-of-relative that had beagles. And he had three that were about twelve weeks old.

Buying beagles is a risky business, even when buying from a relative of a relative. My dad and I went to see the beagles, and we took Nellie my wife along. Buying beagles should include a hunter's spouse to make sure she is equally obligated to take care of them. I knew that if Nellie wasn't in on buying the pups, she might not want to help care for them.

Putting in a little extra effort is worth it to keep from hearing comments like: "You get out there and feed your dogs, you're the one that bought them." The risk of that happening was greatly reduced by taking her with me. Because we were both there when the dogs were bought, then "we" bought them. Not "you" or "I", but "we".

Beagle pups are cute. I watched them for a while, and spotted the two that seemed the most active. Nellie agreed on the selections. We told the uncle of my cousin that we would take the two active ones. Then he showed us a trick.

The uncle held a slice of bread on the outside of the pen, and one pup reached through to grab it. Only thing was, when he closed his mouth on the bread, he also had a fence wire in his mouth. Naturally, when he tried to run off with the slice of bread, the fence didn't move. He assumed something else had ahold of his slice of bread. The other pup was standing nearby, so he assumed the other pup was the culprit. A fight immediately started.

Why, if I had seen this stunt before I gave my word on a deal, I wouldn't have ever bought them. These dogs had obvious behavior problems. The look on my face probably told the owner that I had recognized the brain condition of his dogs.

The man meant no harm to the dogs. To settle the pups down, he gave each of them a small bowl of puppy chow. They seemed happy again. After eating their snack, they had that familiar bulging tummy puppy look. Bulging tummies on a pair of puppies is all it takes for Nellie to fall in love with them. It was a sure sale. I couldn't back out of the deal even if I was willing to go back on my word.

We decided to take our new dogs to my dad's house for the night, then the next day we would head back the 140 miles to my house. It was only a thirty mile drive to Dad's if we took the shortcut. The shortcut was an old blacktop road that had some rough spots between the bigger chuck holes. But it was shorter than the highway and a scenic drive. With all the curves, we couldn't go real fast, so we got to take a good look at the scenery.

The pups had never ridden in a car before. They also had never eaten just before going for a car ride. They didn't seem to mind very much for the first fifteen miles. During the second fifteen miles, they informed us that they were already sick of riding in a car. They didn't say anything. They just threw up the puppy chow they had been given to make their stomachs bulge. Of course, Nellie was holding them when they threw up. She didn't complain too much. By the time we went to bed that night, she had already calmed down.

The following day, we headed out on our 140 miles drive home. The pups had been deprived of food that morning. Things went pretty well for the first 137 miles. Three miles from our destination, they decided they had enough of driving in a car. They used the same technique as the day before to let us know. Both of them got sick on Nellie.

It might seem that Nellie should have gotten very upset, but she couldn't. How could she be upset about two innocent little puppies that she helped select.

Having them home was good. No more need to drive anywhere until it was time to train them. That was a couple of months away.

It was a good feeling. I had my own dogs, and I was ready to start hunting again. They were real dogs this time, even had those all important papers. The lineage was highly thought of by my cousin and his uncle. Couldn't be anything but the best dogs a man could ask for.

Training beagles had always been an easy task. Get them in a field with rabbits, and nature takes over. I found a place to hunt that was crawling alive with rabbits. This would be fun.

Our first trip out was in early October. Season had just started, and it was cool enough to run dogs without making them sick. Ben and Critter didn't have any idea where we were going when I put them in the truck, but it didn't matter to them. They vomited by the time we got to the hunting spot. They were developing an ability to tell when we were almost to the place we were going. They wouldn't throw up too soon, or they would be trapped in their coup with the stuff. Their little pea brained minds were thinking, "Wait until just the right moment, then our hunter friend will get to clean the coup, and we won't have to sit in it."

Even the two conspiring twits I had bought as beagles didn't dampen my spirits. I was on my first rabbit hunt in several years. I had answered the call of the wild. I was back.

The dogs came out of their coups like race horses from the starting gate. They darted around the forty acre field in about 22.6 seconds. Any rabbit they may have passed wouldn't have been disturbed. All it would have seen were a couple of streaks. I had made the mistake of getting these dogs in too good of condition.

Having been worked in the back yard and the field behind us, both dogs were in excellent physical condition. When they returned from their circuit of the forty acres, they weren't even breathing hard. I had hoped the run might slow them down a little, but it didn't appear to have much effect on them. I had become tired just watching.

With both dogs near my side, I headed off down a row of briars. Within twenty yards, I jumped up a rabbit. Neither dog noticed, so I coaxed them to the path, and let them get a good smell. They looked up as if to question why I had them smelling weeds. There wasn't any food there.

We repeated this little routine about eight times in the next two hours. By the eighth time, I was a little short on patience and was helping them get a good whiff of the trail. Picking a beagle up by the nose and tail, it can be stretched in a manner that locates its nose right where you want it. Another technique that works is to hold the dog's tail in your teeth, grasp the snout with one hand and stretch the dog toward the trail. Use the other hand to compress and expand the chest so the dog is known to be getting breaths of air near the trail location. It is a little like working a bagpipe.

Because resorting to scientific approaches as described above didn't seem to be doing much good, I started wishing for the past to return. At least I was hoping that Ernie may be resurrected.

I finally resorted to shooting a rabbit when it jumped up. It was more humane than shooting the dogs, and might do some good. Figured I could show the rabbit to them and let them smell it.

Neither dog bolted when I shot, so at least they weren't gun shy. Either that or they were deaf. I left the rabbit lay where it was shot, and called Ben and Critter to the area. They wandered around for a while. One of them stepped over the poor rabbit in a way that more or less said, "Excuse me, I have to get to the other side."

I finally blew a gasket. These dogs were definitely brain damaged. Perhaps if I threw the rabbit right in front of one of them, he would see it, think it was alive, and attack. The throw was perfect. It skimmed right by Critter's nose and landed about two feet in front of him. Critter jumped back about three feet, now looking at the attack rabbit from a safe distance of five feet. After staring at it for a few seconds to make sure it wasn't going to attack again, he turned and walked away.

Now, I don't give up easily, but I was about out of ideas. One trick was left. It had always worked on previous beagles. I drew my knife and thought about attacking the dogs, but reconsidered and went on to perform the technique that had done so much good for our previous dogs. Instead of attacking the dogs, I removed the heart, lungs, and liver from the rabbit. My previous dogs thought of these parts as delicacies. My handy work with the knife had the attention of my dogs. They both came over to see what I had. Finally, some interest.

I reached out a hand, half expecting to get my fingers taken off as they took the food. I was remembering how one had responded when the fence interfered with his grip on that slice of bread. Both of them stopped a little short. Leaning as far forward as they could, they sniffed to see what it was that I was offering. They both snarled up their lips and turned away. They only liked dry dog food.

At this point, I ran to the truck as fast as I could go. It didn't do any good. Ben and Critter were in such good shape that they were able to keep up with me. I wasn't able to drive away before they got in their coup.

I called my cousin to see if he would know what to do with the brain damaged beagles that his uncle sold me. No offer was made to buy them back. He did suggest a beagle trainer that lived forty miles from my house. Taking them to a trainer was a better idea than going nuts trying to train them myself.

Mr. Melklin said he would train them if they were registered beagles. I assured him they were, but I thought his question was a little strange. The three greatest dogs I ever heard tell of were never registered. The only two brain damaged dogs I ever saw were registered, and he was going to get a chance to train them.

Mr. Melklin drives a hard bargain. He wanted a flat fee for getting them "started". Regardless of whether it took one day or one week. The fee was reasonable because I figured food for the period he would need was going to cost that much.

The evening when I took the dogs to his place, it was dark when I arrived. Mr. Melklin walked out to my truck to remove the pups from their coup. I warned him that they tend to come out of it fast, so he was ready for them. When they came out he grabbed hold. "What in the world is that slimy stuff all over these dogs?"

"Oh, they have a tendency to throw up when they ride in the truck."

"Ya, I've had pukey dogs before. Sure wish you had told me."

Christmas came and went, and I was beginning to think that I may no longer have any beagles. Finally, Mr. Melklin called to say that I could come get them. I asked if they were running rabbits, or had he given up.

When I went to get Ben and Critter, Mr. Melklin offered to put them in the field to see them run. That was a good idea because I hadn't ever seen a brain damaged animal do anything it was supposed to.

They actually did trail something for a while. Both of them barked trail, although I didn't see any rabbits. I asked if they might be false trailing, and I was assured that "those dogs don't have a false bark in them." You can imagine my pleasure in knowing that my dogs could run rabbits. I would get to do some hunting after all.

Five years later, Ben and Critter were still running rabbits and hunting with me. They did their best, and on some days, that wasn't too bad. There were a couple of times that I thought I may have great beagles in the making, and other days when I wondered what had gone wrong in their development. Critter had to retire at twelve, and Ben made it through his last year. They both departed at their thirteenth year.

I haven't seen him in years, but the last time I saw him, Mr. Melklin still had that funny little twitch when I mentioned their names. No, they weren't as good as Lady, Daisy, or Ernie. But they were my beagles, we hunted together more than any other dogs, and they were my friends. Sometimes you need to be able to laugh at your friend's foibles, celebrate when they have successes, and treat them well during all times.

If you can't love a beagle, you can't love anything.

Ernie

ERNIE

Years of rabbit hunting and caring for hounds gave me, at a very young age, the insight and specialized knowledge that placed me in good standing among the outdoorsmen I knew. It is possible that I had a slight case of overconfidence. Whether there was any general overconfidence or not, I saw myself as able to critically and accurately evaluate the beagle breed. From my experience, I began to categorize beagles. The categories were kept simple: the best dog in the world, a great dog, a good hound, an acceptable mutt, and the unfortunate totally inept canine.

Now, it does not take many years of hunting to realize the first reality regarding hunting dogs of any breed. The "best dog in the world" belongs to someone else. The criteria to earn a rating of a "great dog" does include factors that few could ever achieve, so it is not often a hunter can claim to have such an animal in his or her pack. Criteria for "good hounds" is a little less demanding, but certainly still reflects positively on the animal itself and its owner at all times. The "acceptable mutts" typically hunt in the manner expected of them, act like they hear you when you call them, realize a deceased rabbit on the trail is a reason to begin hunting for another rabbit, and generally are completely oblivious to the sound of a firearm. The "inept" does not deserve any more space in this story.

My last two beagles on a normal day fit into the acceptable category and occasionally gave glimpses of moving upward to the good hound designation. On their bad days, well no need to go into details. Anyone that has hunted with a beagle knows they have bad days.

During my life I have complained some about the bad days. In response, dog trainers tried to tell me that the only reason my dogs weren't better was because I didn't run them enough. They had no idea. It wasn't true. Not many hunters would commit to running their dogs as hard as me. I've chased dogs half a mile or more after they lost a rabbit. I've chased them over a mile when they were on the trail of the wrong kind of animal. Nobody runs their dogs any further.

It's not all my fault. It is not always the owner that causes a dog to be less than expected. From the owner's point of view, I believe the responsibility for any problem with a beagle must be shared between the breeder and the trainer. I'm starting to think that possibly the breeder owns the greatest portion of the responsibility, because the genetic makeup of a beagle seems to be a primary factor in his ability to run rabbits. Only the breeder has control over this. I am not a genetics expert, but it is clear from the evidence of the dogs I have encountered, that many dog breeders need to study the subject of genetics a little longer. Those Kennel Association papers don't mean much if the dog doesn't hunt, has the wrong number of legs, or can't smell a skunk. Not once when my dogs were messing up did I pull out their papers and show them that I had proof they could do more.

The hired trainer has not escaped my observations. The trainer is the first person to handle the dog while he is learning to trail rabbits. Life-long habits are formed on that first rabbit trail. I'll expound a little about my one experience with a hired beagle trainer, because that fellow wasn't much brighter than the beagles he was attempting to train. In fact, I think they had outwitted him. Now, to be fair, I know there are very good trainers out there. Just be sure you pick a good one if you want your beagles to be better than acceptable mutts.

Because of the information already shared, an owner of a beagle has much of his destiny with his companion dog already determined before the owner ever gets into the picture. I realize as I write these words that my somewhat critical views of the breeder and trainer are tainted by the last two beagles I owned. Things have been better. Not all my previous dogs were like the last two.

I'll stop with the critical comments about breeders and trainers. The rest of this story is about a very special dog and how special the relationship can become between the master and his companion dog. One of my dogs was a superb animal - perhaps rating between good and great. He was the first beagle that was truly mine. His name was Ernie.

After spending four years in the United States Air Force, I was ready to return home and do some serious hunting with my family. The first step was to get a beagle that knew what to do. As a coming home present, my mother bought a beagle from Ron Chance for $15. Even in 1973, a $15 beagle might be of questionable pedigree. In fact, nobody was quite sure where the young dog came from. We could only judge by size that he might be five or six months old.

Apparently, there wasn't a breeder to mess up Ernie's genes. He was born to an unknown father, and therefore unregistered. As far as that goes, his mother was also unknown. Nobody expected much of him, except me. I was going to be his trainer and his owner. One of the oldest training techniques I know was put to work. I took him hunting.

Having been born under questionable circumstances, Ernie must have sensed that he needed to perform well if he was to compete with the other dogs in the world. It's a little like getting a degree from a small college and going to work among a group of graduates from the University of Illinois. Nobody expects much, but if you don't perform well, you may not be around too long.

The first day I put Ernie in the field, within five minutes he was barking trail on a rabbit. That dog was a natural. I was smiling from ear to ear. I had never seen a beagle start as fast as Ernie. It was clear that he and I would be hunting buddies.

Ernie pushed his first rabbit out of the weeds into a clearing in front of me. I got off a shot with my Fox double barrel that stopped the rabbit. My dad was out of sight of the clearing, so he yelled the normal question. "Did you get it?" I answered with some pride, "Yeah." Then a question with a note of disbelief came back, "Are you sure?" Dad wasn't accustomed to hearing me shoot just one time. All the distraction of the gunshot and subsequent yelling had zero effect on Ernie. He stayed on trail.

Ernie continued to trail right up to the point his nose nudged the rabbit. He looked better on that first rabbit than some of the three year olds I had hunted with. Dad walked up to our location about the time Ernie was approaching the rabbit. There was a little talk about being lucky to get a beagle that started trailing on the first trip. A comparison was made to the luck involved in me getting the first rabbit of the day on the first shot.

Ernie continued to hunt well as we took him on several trips that year. It was obvious that he would be a long term resident at my home. There was a bond that was growing. It grew even stronger as we began hunting alone when my father's health deteriorated and he had to stop hunting.

I know some people hunt with a pack of beagles and they enjoy it. The dogs back one another up. But I only needed Ernie. He didn't need any backup. Rabbits didn't have a hope of shaking him from their trail. Ernie on a trial meant rabbit for supper if I could do my part.

Ernie had a way of doing more than was expected of him. Memories of one particular hunt warm my heart and provide an excellent example of his performance beyond expectation. It was one of our first hunts without my father along. Ernie had been running a rabbit for more than an hour. It was one of those wild rabbits that runs a half mile in one direction before it circles back. It passed me twice, just out of range. I changed locations and the third time it came by, it was about forty yards away. That is a long shot, but I took the shot. It was time to give Ernie the reward of getting the rabbit if I could do the job.

The rabbit rolled and I thought the shot had been good, but it got up and continued on its way. Ernie gave me a funny look as he trailed past. The look made it clear that he was complaining about trailing a rabbit for an hour, then having me miss what he thought was an adequate chance.

But Ernie had heart, and he kept trailing. That rabbit started another one of those long straight runs. He was headed back to some thick stuff where briars and weeds are impenetrable to a human. Well, he made into that briar patch that I really did not want to enter. Ernie went in behind him, and stopped barking trail. When I got to the edge of the thicket, I could see Ernie in there. He had caught the rabbit. I was happy the rabbit had not escaped, but was dreading the effort to get him out of the briars. Then Ernie did the unexpected.

Anyone that ever owned a beagle that would retrieve will understand the level of emotion that I experienced on this trip. Ernie had never given any indication that he was willing to retrieve. But that little beagle picked up the rabbit and brought it out of the thicket to me. I got down on my knees and loved that dog like he was my best friend. He may have been.

Ernie turned out to be more than my hunting dog. He also became a family pet. My oldest daughter (we called her Sam at the time) was about four when we got Ernie. It turned out that Ernie was not only a hunting dog, but he was a child pleaser. He would do anything to make my little girl happy.

She would invent games for Ernie to play, and he would take part as though it was great fun. She sometimes tossed his dog biscuits in a pan of water to see him dive for them. This trick would be repeated until he was full or she ran out of the treats. His sneezing and coughing of water from his nose didn't seem to bother him, and Sam got a good laugh out of it.

She played the same game with him at the Ohio River. It was a deeper dive, but he would give it his best. Anywhere that Sam went, Ernie was willing to go.

The same dog that would go through briars and cut to shreds his ears and tail could act like a baby when the right people were around. We were camping on the Ohio River when he got a wasp sting on a paw. Now, I know that hurt, but he took advantage of the situation. Sam was there to give him attention, so he whined and limped around for several hours. Once he had enough attention, there was a miraculous recovery. That same hot summer day, he went down to a thicket and trailed a rabbit until he was exhausted.

Ernie and I hunted together every day we could as I completed a college degree at Southern Illinois University. When I graduated, my family and I moved to northern Illinois where I took a job teaching school. It was hard, but we temporarily left Ernie with my parents because I didn't have a place to keep him. We lived in an apartment the first couple of years.

It was a terrible separation. Ernie was so upset by the situation that he developed the skills needed to get out of his dog pen and climb out the chain link fence that went around my parents' yard. His repeated efforts got him a reputation of being something of an escape artist. After retrieving my dog about fifty times from various distances, my father urged me to come get my dog.

I was building our first home, and in the back yard I built the best dog pen in the area. It had an insulated dog house, concrete floor, a nice metal frame and wire mesh, and even a wire roof. There was no escape route.

Ernie came home to live with us. We had made it to utopia. My trusted rabbit dog lived at my home, and it was only a short walk from our house to a place where we could hunt. There weren't many rabbits there, but we didn't care. Ernie and I were hunting again.

Circumstances were going to bring change into our lives. Teaching didn't pay enough to meet house payments and feed the family, so I found it necessary to get a job in industry. That moved us to a city. The new job allowed me to pay for a house and buy food, but where we lived wasn't close to any place we could hunt. Ernie and I tried to find a place.

After a few months in the city, rabbit season drew near. I called the department of conservation to find out about available public hunting areas. They sent me some maps.

There were a lot of places, but they were all more than forty miles away. Because I grew up where the furthest hunting spot was about forty miles away, I decided to try the closest available spot. The closest spot contained over two thousand acres. That should be enough.

Ernie was able to sense when I was going to take him hunting. He began getting excited on Wednesday if we were going to hunt on Saturday. I had the same problem. At work, if someone asked me what hardness of lead I was using in my pencil, I might respond that number 6 field loads are adequate. After answering a few questions in that manner, it got to where people didn't ask many questions during hunting season.

Saturday came, and I put Ernie in the front of the car with me. He normally rode in the back, but not today. We had waited too long for this trip, and he deserved better. He understood that he was a dog, and sat patiently in the floor. He sat there and looked at me the whole forty miles. It felt like going on vacation with the kids. His eyes kept asking if we were there yet.

I saw the conservation department sign at the turn-off from the highway. I made the turn onto the blacktop road that runs along the edge of the wildlife area. It looked like the hunting paradise of the world. I was elated, and Ernie was beginning to sense my feelings and developing some of his own. The end of his tail was beginning to circle in happiness.

About a mile down the road, I saw an entrance and a headquarters building. I turned in the entrance, and decided to stop for some advice from one of the area conservation agents. When I stopped the car, Ernie thought it was his cue to get out and hunt. He turned off his self-control and made it a real challenge for me to get out of the car without him. The office was closed, but there were information pamphlets on the door.

As I returned to the car, I noticed the parking lot was full of trucks and trailers. The trucks and trailers were all full of beagles. This was a little upsetting, because I don't care to hunt in a crowded area. I saw one guy get out a dog, and it had on an orange vest with a number. At first, I thought the dog vest might be to prevent the city hunters from shooting the dogs, but the number had me confused.

I had never been around a field trial before, but I finally realized that was what was taking place. Perhaps I could get far enough from them that it wouldn't matter.

I got in the car with a dog that thought it was time to hunt, and read the pamphlet. It had a sentence somewhere on the page that jumped off the paper at me.

HUNTING ONLY ON
MONDAY THROUGH FRIDAY

This was ludicrous. Doesn't the department of conservation know that most people can only hunt on weekends?

If I couldn't hunt here, what was I to do? Could I go somewhere else? I didn't bring the other maps. Two thousand acres had seemed like enough space for one day of hunting. Should I stop somewhere nearby and ask a farmer for permission to hunt rabbits? Not this close to the city. They have surely had too many bad experiences with city hunters. Maybe we could get in on the field trials. Not a chance. Ernie wasn't registered. Just as well. It would have been embarrassing to all those high priced dogs if Ernie emerged the champion.

We would just have to go home. Neither Ernie nor I had ever been through such a miserable experience. The ride back was quiet. Ernie sat in the floor looking at me in disbelief. I couldn't look at him. I was trying to face what I had done by moving to the city to get a job.

The events of that day were probably too much for Ernie's nervous system. He became obsessed with efforts to escape from his dog pen. A solid floor, welded wire mesh side walls and a welded wire mesh roof weren't enough to keep him in. He would twist the wire back and forth with his mouth until he broke the welds. Two or three broken welds and he could push the wire to the side and escape. Once out of his pen, he would look for a place to hunt. Of course he didn't have much luck.

After a couple of years of persistent escape attempts, I figured out that something had to be done. At least one of us should get to hunt. I still needed to earn a living, so I decided to do something for Ernie. It was one of the hardest decisions of my life, and was a mistake.

I took Ernie back to my home town. A friend of my father's knew a farmer that liked to hunt, and he had a nice place to keep a beagle. I gave Ernie to the farmer so he could again live in the country and hunt when he wanted to. I did it for Ernie, and thought it was the best way to let him do what he loved so much. As much as I thought it needed to be done, it felt like I was giving up a member of the family. But it was done, and I had to explain to Sam. We headed home without our little friend in the car with us. My wife, daughters and I all cried as we drove home that day.

As much as I still wish I had made a better decision, I am pleased to think that Ernie, the greatest beagle I ever owned, got to hunt his last few years.

After I gave Ernie away, I realized that I had the same urge to escape that he had demonstrated. That dog and I were more alike than I had realized. Maybe he had it right and I was the one that was a little off on the logic. I came to recognize that the things we love to do in life should have some impact on where we live and what we do with our time. That little dog had been my hunting buddy and companion to my girls. He had also taught me something about living my life.

About two years after Ernie had gone, I came to a point where I needed to make a decision. One of two things must take place. Find a way to hunt from where I lived, or move to a place where I could hunt and learn to live on what I could make in that location. Things worked out. I found a pretty good compromise. I moved a short distance from the city and found some pretty good hunting places within a short drive of my home. I got a couple of beagles that never achieved the status of Ernie, but on a good day they were acceptable. We hunted for thirteen years, and I am glad that we did.

There will never be another Ernie in my life, but I certainly hope that every hunter will have at least one dog like him. They are rare. If you get one, find a way to keep him.

On Point

WILDLIFE ESTIMATOR

I am truly impressed with the conservation department in my state. The founders of this outstanding department had the foresight to recognize the need to maintain and improve our wildlife resources and sporting opportunities. All their practices impress me, except one. That one practice is the fine art of wildlife estimation, which could be greatly improved by using methods I have witnessed during my years of experience.

As unbelievable as it may be, the state resorted to what they consider scientific methods of determining wildlife populations. I suppose the need to determine wildlife populations must have been schedule-critical for some unknown reason, because they implemented their counting methods without talking to me or any of my associates. All experienced hunters and fishermen know that wildlife estimation is an art form that can only be perfected after many years of hunting or fishing with a master hunter or fisherman. No scientific method could compare with the methods I've witnessed.

I am unaware of any university teaching the fine art of wildlife estimating as part of their conservation programs. At least the art is not taught in the form that I am accustomed. If wildlife estimating is taught at all, I imagine they, like the department of conservation, attempt to convert the art of estimation into a scientific process. Having attended a university for a few years, I would expect such a thing from them.

Let me provide at least one story to demonstrate problems with the scientific approach for determining wildlife populations. Consider the example of how conservation agents sometimes estimate fish populations by using electricity to stun the fish. The stunned fish rise to the top of the water where they can be counted. After a while, the fish are thought to recover and swim away.

If the fish do actually recover, they will probably never be the same and of little value to the sportsman. Figure it out. Put yourself in the fish's position. First a fish hears a boat, then he gets the living daylights shocked out of him. Any fish big enough to eat is surely smart enough to get out of the area the next time he hears a boat.

If making a nervous wreck out of the fish isn't enough of a reason to discourage a scientific approach like this, perhaps the legality of the process should be considered. Conservation agents using these methods are apparently unaware that they are doing something that sportsmen are prohibited from doing. A sportsman cannot shock fish. It is against the law.

I am aware of the law on this matter because of what happened one summer when I was a boy. A somewhat seedy man, that I was somewhat acquainted with, was said to be using electricity to shock fish to the top. He used a different method of counting fish than does the conservation department. In his approach to this he would put them in his boat, and count them as he cleaned them back at his dock. Anyway, I heard that he was found out and was arrested for counting fish in this manner.

Rather than have our agents subjected to being arrested for trying to do their job, I recommend they use the methods of fish estimation that have been passed down from one fisherman to another. It works well once you fully understand how to interpret events that follow the initial estimation. To get good at it takes some time.

Wildlife estimation is easiest to learn from an old-timer. However, even with the guidance of an old-timer, the learning process can take several years. For a slow learner, it could take decades. Attempting to learn from trial-and-error is not recommended. It can be frustrating, and might lead a person to believe that wildlife estimation is inaccurate.

My father taught me the lessons that he learned from his brother Robert and Ed Manhart, a master-fisherman at Rosiclare, Illinois. Their methods were very simple. A person only need to develop the ability to read the signs (modern fishermen call these things "structure"). It is also helpful to understand quantitative fishing terms such as: bunch, mess, lot, and none. The first three mean there are enough fish. The last means there isn't any point in fishing here.

Every fishing trip with my father was a learning experience. Each time we went to put our trotlines in the Ohio River, fish population estimates were required. The estimates were made without much fanfare or formality, but the message and count were always clearly stated. Our boat would slow at some point along the river, and my dad would announce that this spot looked good. It may sound like this, "There's got to be a mess of fish here."

The water on that particular stretch of the river must have had just the right appearance at the moment Dad looked at it. My brother and I would look at each other, then look at Dad and agree that it also looked good to us. One of the first things I learned about wildlife estimation is to agree with the people having the most experience. They may not take you along for another lesson if you question their judgment.

After watching and listening to more experienced estimators, I was sure that I could learn to make estimates as accurate as anyone else. It took a while to learn the techniques used by the master estimators. Part of the learning process was to recognize the importance of not speaking too soon while learning. The best process was to simply slow the boat and see if a more knowledgeable person would speak up. I would occasionally slow the boat and listen.

Someone would say, "Nope, there's not going to be anything here."

Time to speed up the boat. If timed correctly, this can be done as though the estimate was only a confirmation of a decision already made by the pilot.

Sometimes, as we motored the boat down the river, someone would point at a place along the bank. Slowing the boat upon seeing a pointed finger results in an estimate that goes something like this, "There's bound to be a mess of fish in that place." As an apprentice estimator, this was a good time to stop the boat and prepare to put in a trotline.

It was amazing. The next morning, our trotlines would either have fish on them — or they wouldn't. Both situations proved there had been a mess of fish exactly where the master estimator had indicated. If you caught fish, you knew they were there because you could see them. If you didn't catch fish, you also knew they were there but not biting.

Several things could cause them not to bite. One was the river flowing too quickly. It might have even been because of a barometric pressure change. Another possible cause was a wind out of the east. Other similar reasons do exist, and most master estimators have a complete list of reasons they are on occasion willing to share.

Nobody that ever fished with us ever doubted that our fish estimating ability was accurate. They understood that we had the trained eyes and senses of master estimators. It was amazing.

The estimating processes used for fishing are not exactly the same for upland game, but there are some similarities.

The fish estimating ability of my family was impressive, but even more developed was our ability to estimate the rabbit and quail populations in southern Illinois. I've had the good fortune to be able to apply these same talents in Missouri over a few decades.

Upland game populations, deer and waterfowl are not measured in the same quantitative terms as fish. They are estimated in quantities such as: several, lot, gobs, little herd, large herd, small covey, large covey, small flock, large flock, and none. Places containing none are not hunted. All others may be hunted, depending on the level of patience and amount of time the hunter has.

Quail, of course, are measured in coveys. Covey size ranges from a pair of birds (a small covey) up to a hundred or so (a large covey). There may be no coveys, maybe one covey, a few coveys, or several coveys. Unfortunately the decline in quail populations results in most estimates today being one or two small to medium size coveys.

For the experienced hunter, it is possible to estimate rabbit and bird populations simply by driving down a country road. A field full of weeds with a few brush piles at the side can automatically be sized up for wildlife content by a good hunter. Seldom will a good hunter be wrong about a wildlife estimate. By the way, don't tell a good hunter that his game estimates have been in error while the two of you are still hunting.

There have been many times when we stopped at a farmhouse to get permission to hunt after an expert estimator announced that a field appeared to have a lot of rabbits. Sometimes we harvest a couple of rabbits at these locations, and sometimes we get several. I don't recall ever getting more than the quantity the estimator determined to be present. This seems to be adequate proof that our estimates are relatively accurate.

Sometimes we don't get anywhere near the quantity the estimator knows to be in the field. There are explanations for this, and the estimator is usually willing to provide at least one reason if asked. The reason may be a problem with the dogs. It seems that dogs have days when their noses are cold. A dog with a cold nose couldn't track a skunk on a damp morning. Another common problem is that rabbits will go in holes. This reason has been given by my ex-brother-in-law's friend on days when I am sure the rabbits closed the holes behind them. They must have, because I didn't see any holes during a full day of hunting.

I've already mentioned that the quail population is down, but quail estimating remains an art. The most challenging part is estimating the number of birds in a covey. I am still working on this. The oldest person in the hunting party is usually the one that estimates bird counts the best. An exception to this can occur if only one hunter owns bird dogs. He is then the best estimator.

No apprentice estimator challenges a bird estimate unless he wants to learn on his own from then on. A bird count never looks the same to any two people, because everyone has a different viewpoint of the covey as it comes up from the ground.

The oldest hunter usually has the most experience in seeing birds come up, so it is logical that the older person has the best chance of getting the estimate correct. Of course, there are exceptions. Young hunters on their first few trips have a relatively good chance of estimating the same number of birds as the oldest hunter. Only the new hunters and the older ones are likely to get the count high enough.

The first covey of quail I jumped nearly scared me to death. I was a small boy, and the amount of noise they made was proof that a large covey had just risen. I am sure that I flushed at least fifty or sixty birds. After adding another ten birds to make sure I hadn't missed any, I announced the size of the covey (seventy). Nobody disagreed.

My dad got two birds on that first rise, and our champion birddog hunted for hours to point five singles that day. Dad said we should leave the rest for seed. Sixty three birds seemed like enough for seed.

I have never seen another covey as large as that first one. However, my nephews have. They always seemed to have a better viewing angle than me when we jumped quail. I saw about half as many as they did. Some people hunting with us didn't even see as many as I did. They didn't actually say it, but they looked at us a little funny.

Yes, accurate quail estimates are the most difficult wildlife estimates to make. The only way to get real good at it is to spend a lot of time in the field, then report what you have seen at a hunting club. It is amazing how many birds you can recall seeing when telling stories at the club.

Large game animals also need to be estimated. Deer populations have increased for several decades, and estimating abilities for deer can be developed to a level that is very impressive to family members and friends. I've worked hard on my ability as an estimator of deer populations. My wife Nellie and our two daughters are often amazed with my ability in this area.

For years I had the pleasure of going to my small farm, where I sometimes saw deer moving through the field or woods. More often, I only saw the tracks where the deer travelled. When I arrived home from a trip to the farm, I was able to relay to my family a story about the size of the deer herd that was using the area. A single set of tracks can provide a lot of information to an experienced estimator.

With the deer herd increasing in size, it is common to see deer when driving through the country. These occasions are good times to hone my estimating ability. It is possible to count the deer if I see them for one or two seconds and there are fewer than fifty of them. A larger herd may require a more general estimate.

I recently saw a television advertisement that gave me the perfect opportunity to show my family just how quickly I can estimate a deer herd. The advertisement showed a snapshot camera on the bottom half of the TV screen. On the top half, a herd of whitetail bucks was shown. The announcer said the camera sold for under thirty bucks.

I quickly looked at the TV and announced that it looked like there must be at least fifty deer in the picture. My family was impressed.

Boat Launch

BOATING FOIBLES

Every boy should be fortunate enough to have an adult role model. I had one in my father. I realize that I had a biased point of view, but as far as could be determined by me, Dad was one of the most knowledgeable sportsmen around. Everything we needed to do, he could get done. He knew how to get bait that always caught fish, made our first river Jon boat, made our trotlines and dip nets, and usually caught fish regardless of how well anyone else was doing.

Among the long list of things he did well was an essential act of launching a boat. Many others were impressed by his ability at this, and more than once I saw him put a boat in the water for someone who was struggling to get the job done. He wouldn't barge in and take over, but if he watched someone make five or ten attempts, get out of their car and speak in foreign languages that I did not understand, and drop to their knees and look to the sky; Dad would nicely ask if they would like some help. Sixty seconds later, their boat was in the water. They would be amazed and shower praise upon him. He would just smile and offer to take their boat back out if we were around when they were ready to leave.

He didn't try to make anyone look bad, but fishing with him made much of the rest of the world a little comical. It's not that anyone else was dumber than us, because I am sure they were smart people. It was just that they didn't appear to have been taught or didn't have enough experience. Dad taught me that it isn't nice to make fun of other people's problems or limitations, but the things that happen on boat ramps cannot be seen as anything but humorous – assuming they don't get hurt.

Launching a boat was one of those things my dad mastered before I entered this world. He could back a boat trailer down a path with no more than a few inches of space on each side of the trailer. Anywhere there was water deep enough for our boat, he could find a way to get the boat to it. The toughest job I saw pulled off was launching the boat from a levy that had a road down the top of it. The road was only one lane wide, but that didn't stop our crew. The boat was launched and the car moved to a proper place for parking without even a slight interruption in the traffic on the levy.

When a boy or girl is taught to launch a boat by a father that is such an expert, a new boat launching expert is developed that has a great deal of ability and knowledge. Once this vast knowledge of boat launching is acquired, a visit to a launch ramp can be interesting, possibly entertaining. This is especially true when a crowd of newcomers are at the ramp.

Newcomers can be rather easily spotted. They usually have the boat trailer halfway between the top of the ramp and the water, and it is at a 90° angle to the ramp and parallel to the water's edge. If they pull the car forward to realign the car and trailer, the next attempt at backing the trailer is sure to result in the trailer being oriented in the opposite direction from the previous attempt. However, it is unlikely to be any closer to the water.

Anytime a newcomer is seen in the above predicament, the best thing to do is park your car and pour a cup of coffee from the thermos. Sit back and wait. Offering to help is pointless if the offer is made before the previously explained display of behavior. The newcomer will not yet realize any need for assistance.

If the ramp is wide enough for two boats to be launched, do not attempt to use it if a newcomer is already on it. Attempting to back your boat trailer down an adjacent position on the ramp exposes your car, boat and trailer to high risk for damage.

Usually, at the fourth or fifth attempt by a newcomer to back the trailer down a ramp, a second member of the newcomer party will offer to replace the current driver of the car. This may happen at the second or third attempt if the newcomer's wife is driving during the first attempts. It's not that women are any worse at backing trailers down ramps. Husbands are more impatient. It should be noted here that if one newcomer replaces another as driver, the attempt count is reset to zero.

After the third or fourth try by the second driver, someone from a different group of newcomers may offer to drive. Newcomers are anxious to help one another. Besides, newcomers are always eager to back their trailer down the ramp and don't like to wait on other newcomers that may be in front of them. Once again, a change of the driver resets the attempt counter. Only after five to ten attempts and a little time on their knees will a newcomer welcome assistance from an expert.

Within thirty or forty minutes, a group of newcomers can usually get their trailer to the edge of the water. If they do succeed, it is at the moment of success that everyone in the newcomer's party remembers they didn't put their things in the boat. Some of them aren't even aware that you are supposed to load your boat before getting on the ramp. Relax and continue to watch. Loading the boat while partially over water will take no more than five to ten minutes.

By the time all this takes place, twenty boat owners are lined up to launch their boats. Five of us are sitting in lawn chairs watching the entire procession. That's how you spot the experienced boat launchers. They know to bring lawn chairs.

There was a day when the activities of one group of newcomers stood out far more than all the others. The following is an account of that series of events.

Just because a newcomer family gets their boat in the water does not mean everything is good to go. Stay in your lawn chair until the boat is launched, operational, and the launch vehicle moved off the ramp.

Upon our arrival at the boat ramp, the newcomer trailer was located across the top of the ramp and parked for loading. Life-jackets, coolers, skis, ropes, fire extinguishers, flashlights, and one six-year-old are all loaded into the boat. Well, things are looking up because the boat was loaded before launching. As before, five experienced boaters arrive while the newcomers are loading. Two of the experienced boaters head for a shade tree with their lawn chairs. The other three prove themselves to be less than expert and perhaps a little impatient. They begin to give the newcomers hand signals to help them get their boat backed into the water. Some of the hand signals didn't seem to have anything to do with the direction to move the boat, because they only used one finger that was mostly pointed up. Hopefully that won't happen again, because it caused a lot of shouting and delayed the launching effort.

Finally, everything started to look good. The back of the boat was floated from the trailer and the car was stopped before it was in the water. The car motor was left running to make it easy to get the car off the ramp as soon as the boat was launched. This wasn't an attempt to clear the ramp for the line of boaters waiting. It was instead an attempt to hurry the process to get the car and trailer parked to allow all the newcomers to be in the boat before it cast off for an adventure.

The transmission of the car was placed in neutral to prevent the car from taking off without the driver. The driver started to get out to release the boat - whoops; don't forget to set the emergency brake and use wheel chocks.

All members of the newcomer group were understandably excited. Their boat had started to float, and the six year old was beaming because she was the only one to feel their new boat float. If you recall, she was loaded in the boat while at the top of the ramp. Kids love to ride in the boat on the ramp, even if it is extremely dangerous. If you don't know why, just don't do it.

The father in their family made his way to the winch and released the rope from the bow hook. One good push and the boat started rolling off the trailer.

Three seconds later, a couple of thoughts passed through the father's mind. He was standing on the boat ramp as the boat floated freely from the trailer. First thought: The boat really looks good on the water. This was a combined feeling of success and pride of ownership. Second thought: Nobody had hold of a rope that was tied to any part of the boat.

A flash of panic hit, but it appeared to be quickly brought under control – no problem. Father was a quick thinker and had it figured out. He called out for the little girl to throw him a rope. Upon his request, the little girl did exactly as she was told. She reached down and picked up the rope that was earlier moved from the car to the boat. With all her might she threw it toward her father. It was still coiled in a nice bundle when he caught it.

The little girl in the boat was starting to think faster than the adults on the shore. She realized that she was on her own. Panic set in. It was a panic much like the perpetual hysteria that so often strikes sportsmen when they have a dilemma. What else could she do? She shrieked. A loud and sustained wailing nose was heard back in town. People there started going to their storm shelters. All the experienced boat launchers got out of their lawn chairs and were lined up watching and wondering what could possibly happen next.

The type of hysteria demonstrated by the little girl has a tendency to spread, and it did spread into the entire group of newcomers. Everyone was bouncing up and down with arms and legs flailing and some of them were shrieking while others were speaking in a strange language. The father quickly came to his senses and made a mad dash for the boat. He dropped everything that he was holding (including the rope), lunged forward, and in about two steps was swimming with his shoes on and his wallet still in his pants. He reached the boat and climbed aboard, much to the little girl's relief.

The hysteria subsided and everyone relaxed. The father had taken control of the situation. The experienced group of boat launchers sat back down on their lawn chairs. Perhaps the best thing for the father to do was paddle the boat back to shore. Let's recall the inventory of things put in the boat while it was on the ramp a little earlier. There were: Life-jackets, coolers, skis, ropes, fire extinguishers, flashlights, and one six year old. Funny, no paddle.

He was already wet, so he jumped back out and tried to swim while holding to the side of the boat. It took a lot of effort and more than a little time to pull a twenty foot inboard/outboard for 10 yards or so. Seems the motor would have been faster.

When the boat was only a few yards from the dock, the little girl began complaining about her feet getting wet. She looked around and reported that a hole at the back of the boat was leaking. It was a nice round hole that looked like it was made at the factory. It even had a little chrome fitting in it. Imagine that, designing a boat so that it leaked. Best thing to do was take the boat back out of the water and return it to the dealer. Maybe they had one that would be less trouble.

Well, boating entertainment is not limited to newcomers on boat ramps. Speedboat drivers are nearly as interesting as newcomers. This was definitely the case when they showed up at a launch ramp that was normally used by fishermen.

Speedboaters have a natural tendency to think everyone is impressed by the speed of their boats. It's sort of like brain-damaged pickup drivers that slalom through traffic as though they are in a race. Actually, most fishermen are impressed when the speedboaters go by with their female friends wearing skimpy swimsuits. Of course, the crazy way they drive their boats also catches their attention.

Some areas in the south end of Frog Lake weren't very deep, and in other areas where it was deep, it still had most of a forest under the surface. Very few people used the south end of the lake for anything other than fishing. Because of a combination of shallow areas and submerged trees, speed boating was not safe there.

We sometimes fished this part of the lake for bluegill and crappie. Most of a day could be spent there without anyone going past in a big hurry. Fishermen understood that when someone is anchored in a spot fishing, it isn't good manners to go past with a big wake trailing behind. Because of this common understanding, most fishermen will give a wide berth to others or slow down to avoid creating a wake.

A new speedboat could be spotted at the fishing launch ramp every once in a while. The fishermen in sight of the ramp would all shake their heads in disbelief, and grin. That may be a sign that new boat owners should be told about. If there are crusty old fishermen around grinning as you launch your boat, ask them about the water depth and submerged structure.

Everyone would stop fishing for a while, because a replay of previous events was about to take place. The speedboater put his new craft in the water, and then he began to cruise a circuit to show each of the fishermen his new boat. He pretended to be interested in determining whether everyone was catching fish.

He went at a speed that threw up the maximum size wake, you know, just at a speed prior to the boat rising up to plane on the surface of the water. While going at this speed, he approached to within fifteen feet of each fisherman's boat and asked the same question. "Are you catching any?" At this distance he could hear their answer, and maybe the fisherman could get a good look at his new boat.

Everyone may have a boat half full of fish, but they gave him the same answer. "Not doin' much good." The fishermen had a funny grin on their faces. The speedboater smiled, apparently pleased with the fisherman's good spirits, and waved as he headed off for the next fishing boat.

If he was really lucky and made it around the circuit to all the boats in sight, he would then pull out a few feet from the last boat and show off a little. He would push the throttle control forward, and his boat would in most cases surge forward for a distance of perhaps 100 yards before it happened. Then a tree stump would reach up and grab the lower unit on his motor. It was a strange sound, but one that could not be mistaken. The motor would be shut down and the disabled speedboat settled on the water's surface. The fishermen shook their heads slightly, and went back to fishing. One of them would help the speedboater a little later, but for now the waters were calm and it was time to fish.

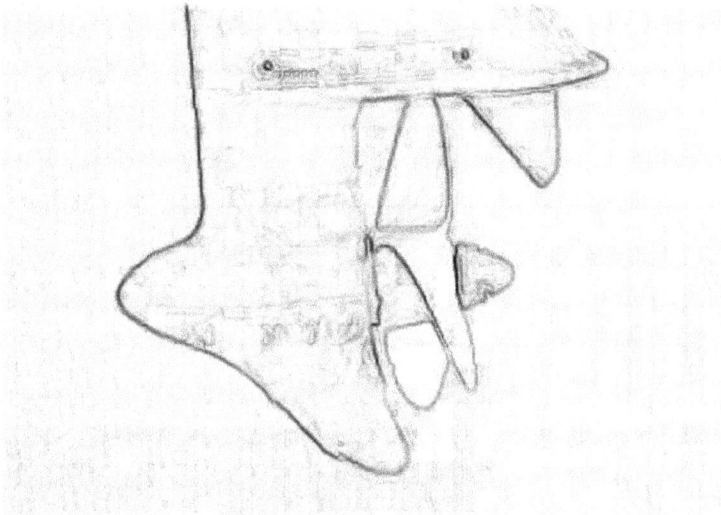

Sea King 22HP

SHEAR PINS

Invention of outboard boat motors made it relatively easy for fishermen to travel long distances across water to reach a favorite fishing location. The inventors of the outboard motor seemed to have thought of everything. They came up with a device to prevent complete destruction of the lower unit and driveshaft when a fisherman tries to cross submerged logs, stumps, and rocks. The device is called a shear pin.

As beneficial as the shear pin can be, it can also become a nuisance that ruins a person's entire outlook on boating. This is not an unusual situation. There are all types of machines that are a benefit to us, but putting them to work sometimes has negative impacts. Take the automobile as an example. It is one of the machines that over the past 100 years greatly impacted our ability to travel between locations. It is great when it works like it is supposed to. It can become the source of great anguish when not working correctly.

Everyone who owns an outboard boat motor probably knows what a shear pin is. Now, to be fair, people that own newer motors may have never seen a shear pin. Newer designs have omitted this device, and the detrimental impact of that omission is yet to the determined. Regardless of the recent changes in outboard motor design, a shear pin is a small metal rod (a pin) that extends through a hole in the motor drive shaft. The pin is long enough to extend out both sides of the shaft and go into a groove in the propeller.

The purpose of the shear pin is to transmit power from the drive shaft to the propeller so that the shaft and propeller turn at the same speed. Should the propeller suddenly stop on something like a submerged log, the shear pin is supposed to break (shear) to prevent ruining the drive shaft. The idea is that the shaft can continue to rotate when the propeller has been stopped by something solid, and that prevents bending the drive shaft or ruining gears.

If outboard motors were made with the propeller firmly attached to the drive shaft, the drive shaft would bend or break the first time the propeller hit something solid like a log, stump or rock. Fortunately, the shaft of an outboard will not be bent or broken if the motor has a correctly made shear pin. A pin that is of the correct diameter and material will break when the propeller hits a solid object. So, when a shear pin breaks, the propeller is free to spin on the shaft or to stand still while the shaft spins. In other words, there is no rotational power transmitted between the shaft and the propeller.

It should be noted that, as important as shearing the pin is in regard to saving a boat motor from damage, once the pin is sheared, it is impossible to propel the boat until the shear pin is replaced. You're stuck.

Replacement of a shear pin was intended by designers to be an easy task, but that is not the way it always works out. Depending on many factors that are not influenced by the design engineer, the actual level of difficulty associated with replacement of a shear pin can range from very simple to darn near impossible. The level of difficulty has nothing to do with the manufacturer. One model of outboard is just about the same as any other when it comes to changing shear pins. Changing a shear pin on a Brand X outboard may take two minutes on a good day, and then take three hours the very next time.

It's been my observation that a few factors impact the level of difficulty. One factor affecting difficulty is your location at the time you need to make the replacement. If you are five miles from the boat ramp, things are going to be far more difficult than if a quarter mile from the ramp. Another factor is how big of a hurry you are in. When there is no reason at all to hurry along, the replacement will typically be without difficulty. When a storm is moving in and your safety is at risk, a more challenging replacement should be expected.

Shear pin replacement is easiest when your boat is located in your garage. It is almost certain that the propeller will slip right off the drive shaft when the retention nut is removed. With the propeller removed, the pin will slide out of its hole as easily as the manufacturer meant for it to happen. The only situation where a garage replacement is difficult is when you are in a hurry. If two buddies are waiting for you to pick them up for a fishing trip, and you decide to replace an old pin that may be worn, problems are bound to occur.

A problem pin change goes something like this. When the propeller is slipped off the shaft, the pin doesn't quite look right. The ends are slightly bent. That stump you hit the other day almost sheared the pin, and that is why it's bent. A push on the pin doesn't cause it to slide out of the hole, because a bent pin does not slide through a straight hole. A hammer on the end of the pin hardly moves it. In fact, after hitting it a few times the pin is now jammed tighter in the hole and the end of the pin is mushroomed so that it will never pass through the hole. A hacksaw, file and punch are employed and thirty minutes later the pin is out of the shaft.

A garage repair such as the one described in the preceding paragraph is almost certain to result in a lakeside shear pin replacement within 5 minutes of getting to the fishing hole. This has to do with the probability of shear pin breakage. There is a reverse relationship between the time to the next breakage and the amount of effort put into the last replacement. If the last pin was nearly impossible to replace, a very short time to the next replacement should be expected.

Shear pin replacement while on water is always more difficult than a garage replacement.

A trip across a lake that is filled with old tree stumps gives a person a good chance to investigate the difficulties involved with shear pin replacement while on water. If the boat isn't heavily loaded, and all of the fishing for the morning has been completed, the replacement may go fairly well. If only one other person is in the boat, you have the best chance for success. More people will offer too much advice, and one of them is too likely to mention that he is in a hurry. Anyone in the boat that is in a hurry will ruin the chances for an easy replacement. When things are perfect and all the stars are properly aligned, all that needs to be done is to tilt the motor up, reach back over the water, and complete all the necessary operations.

The process goes like this. Remove the cotter pin and place it in the boat. Unscrew the retention nut and place it in the boat. Lift off the propeller and place it in the boat. The shear pin pieces will slip out of the shaft and fall in the water with any luck at all. Slip in a new pin and hold it in place as you place the propeller over the shaft and down onto the pin. CAUTION: Be careful not to drop anything in the water. Did you notice that I avoided the D word in that caution? You would be doomed if I had said don't do something. Continuing on, thread the retention nut back on the shaft, then insert the cotter pin and bend the ends of the cotter pin. If all the above was successfully accomplished, you have completed the best possible over-water replacement. Your chances of success were about as good as winning the state lottery. You should celebrate – but only after getting all the way back to the boat ramp. Don't celebrate too soon.

I once experienced the best possible over-water replacement. All other shear pin events have been different. In fact, I will never attempt another over-water replacement.

A more conservative, but difficult approach to shear pin replacement was adopted many years ago. I take the motor off the transom and pull the motor in the boat with me, then I work on it. It takes more time and effort this way, but I get to keep all my outboard motor parts, even if I drop one. The motor is even secured to the boat using a lanyard. Dropping a motor in the water is not good. Dropping it in the water without a lanyard is very expensive.

My reasons for abandoning the attempt for another perfect over the water replacement is one effort that went bad. Our boat was full of camping gear (tent, cots, food, fishing equipment, everything), my dad, brother and me. We were headed for a camping spot about three miles down the Ohio River, and a thunderstorm was about to move into our area. My brother was piloting the boat at the time. We were about 150 feet from the

Illinois bank. The water was perhaps thirty feet deep and there should be no risk other than a rare submerged log.

Our motor lurched and made an awful sound that means the shear pin just broke. An underwater log (a sinker) had found us. The law of shear pin probability should have told us that we didn't have a chance of making a successful trip to our downstream camping spot. The same laws should have also warned that an over the water replacement would be impossible on that day.

There was a whole list of reasons that should have indicated we would have problems. We were going to a special camping spot, we were heavily loaded, we had three people in the boat, evening was approaching, a storm was approaching, we were in deep water, and most importantly of all; we were running in open water that we knew was as safe as anywhere could be. Based on Wilson's Law of Shear Pin Probability, breaking a shear pin was approximately 99.9% probable.

Between the three of us, we had many years of experience and knew what to do, but we were in a hurry. There was no time to waste. We had to put up camp, bait the trotlines and put them out before dark came or the storm got to us. All three people in the boat were experienced at shear pin replacement, so there would be plenty of advice.

Brother John began the operation on the shear pin. He tilted the motor up to expose the propeller. The first piece of advice was offered by my father. "You had better pull the motor up in the boat with you." That was almost as bad as using the D word.

Well, now that advice was given, pulling the motor into the boat was certain not to happen. Being the youngest in the boat, I knew to keep my mouth shut. I also knew my brother. He wasn't about to pull the motor into the boat after being told to.

The cotter pin was successfully removed from the retention nut and placed in the boat. Of course, safe retrieval of the cotter pin didn't matter because we always had spare cotter pins. Nothing is ever lost if you carry spares. Next, the retention nut was taken loose and placed in the boat. The propeller should now slide off.

John was the strongest person I knew, but try as hard as he could, the propeller would not slide from the shaft. We all assumed the pin had smeared around the shaft when it sheared. The propeller wouldn't budge. Several attempts were made at prying the propeller off with a screwdriver. That didn't work. It was wobbled back and forth to see if it could be worked off the shaft a little at a time. That didn't work.

John announced, "Looks like the motor will have to be pulled into the boat to make it easier to get at that problem propeller." Now that he came to this conclusion on his own, it would be okay to put the motor in the boat. As my brother started to tilt the motor back down to loosen the motor clamps, my father offered another piece of advice. "Put the retention nut back on to make sure the propeller doesn't come off in the water." No way. It couldn't possibly come off if John couldn't get it loose.

As the motor tilted back down, the propeller could be seen sliding off the end of the shaft. The water had applied an even force across the entire propeller and gently lifted it from the shaft. Of course, once free of the shaft, gravity took over and it went toward the river bottom rather quickly. John watched the couple of seconds until it was out of sight. Two seconds can sometimes seem like an eternity. This was one of those times. After a few moments of hysteria, anchors were put overboard to hold our position.

We aren't stupid people. We would simply put the spare propeller on the motor. Hummm, it wasn't in its usual place. Oh yeah, we decided that we had hauled that thing with us for five years and were tired of hauling around the extra weight. We never seemed to need it, anyway.

Several diving attempts by my brother didn't result in bringing the propeller to the surface. He decided to give up when lightning struck somewhere downstream. He said the electrical charge was quite exhilarating. Whether or not he actually felt anything wasn't important. All three of us knew it was time to head for shore with a thunderstorm closing in on us.

We rowed back upstream to where we usually camped. Yes, we did still carry oars with us just in case they were ever needed. Once to shore, Dad and I agreed that John could drive the 75 miles back home to get the other propeller. Meantime, Dad and I used the oars to put our trotlines in the river. We also set up camp and had supper ready by the time John returned.

Our fishing trip turned out to be a success, and I even learned a valuable lesson about changing shear pins. I have never again attempted an over the water shear pin replacement.

When I changed a shear pin on a lake or river, people going past gave me funny looks. I guess they weren't accustomed to seeing a man with his outboard motor in the boat with him. The protective net around me and my equipment may have also looked a little strange.

Having changed several shear pins, I've been able to develop an ability to know when I will need to change another one and to predict the difficulty of making the change. The situation in which my brother managed to lose the propeller was approximately the most likely possible situation for causing a shear pin to be broken. We were in a hurry, it had been months since the last shear pin broke, more than one other person was in the boat, a thunderstorm was about to hit, our trotlines weren't in the water yet, and we didn't have a spare propeller. The only things that could have made breaking a pin more likely would have been more missing parts or an absence of tools. If I were to find myself in the same situation as that day, I would know that a shear pin would break and that it would be nearly impossible to change. I would stay off the water on such a day.

The above described experience and a couple of additional boating trips that stand out in my memory have prepared me for the worst possible set of events. On one trip, my cousin Claude and I took our wives with us to scout a new lake for a good duck hunting location. I was still a young man and didn't have the experience to know it at the time, but spectators in a boat are a certain cause for breaking a shear pin. I learned that it can also complicate the replacement.

During the first half of our outing, I had impressed everyone with my ability to maneuver my father's boat through the fallen tree tops and logs on the lake. We made our way to what looked like an ideal spot for future hunts and started to turn around.

After turning the boat, it happened. There was a submerged structure that had a slot that was approximately five inches wide and perfect for the lower housing of the motor to pass through. The slot couldn't be seen from above water. I couldn't have aimed for it if I wanted to, but sometimes fate ensures that certain events take place. The lower unit went into that opening, but of course the propeller could not pass through. It caught on the sides of the slot and abruptly stopped spinning. The chances were one in a million for most people. For me, it was 999,999 in a million. The shear pin had broken.

Considering that a shear pin was broken, everything else about the situation appeared to be as good as could be expected. I had spare shear pins and tools in the boat. Unbelievable as it may seem, I was within twenty feet of the shore. I would just paddle the boat to shore, get out, and replace the pin.

I paddled the boat over to the shore. To keep things simple, I put on my hip boots and started to get out to replace the pin. The boat was only fourteen feet long, so the water at the back of the boat was probably fifteen to eighteen inches deep. I started to step over the side of the boat at the back. I was in a bit of a hurry to get the pin replaced so that we could get back to the launch ramp and enjoy our picnic. I stepped out rather quickly. I was straddling the side of the boat as my overboard leg continued to go down, down, down. My foot never did touch bottom. My downward movement was stopped when my crotch was firmly against the side rail of the boat.

Claude's wife got a lot of amusement out of the facial expressions I made at that time. She laughed and laughed. I didn't make any noises, but I did worry about my daughter being an only child.

After a short recovery period, I decided to turn the back of the boat to shore and change the shear pin on dry land. This worked out, and we were headed back to the launch ramp as darkness closed in. Returning after dark wasn't a real problem because the boat was flexible enough to bounce off the sides of the few trees that were in the lake. Getting back a little late didn't turn out to be a big problem because I was capable of cooking hamburgers for our picnic in complete darkness. We also ate in darkness. No need for my guests looking too closely at those burgers. Now that I think about it, I believe that was the last time Claude and his wife were in a boat or on a picnic with me.

A person that owns a motor with a shear pin in it can do little to avoid an occasional shear pin replacement. The best thing to do is be prepared for the possibility of a need to replace a pin. That, in itself, will reduce the number of times you will actually need to do it. Should a time come where you must replace a pin, if at all possible, move to dry land before taking anything loose from the boat or motor. That alone will probably cause the procedure to go smoothly. Any other approach, and anything can happen.

Good luck.

Counting Birds

FRIENDLY COMPETITION

Hunting, fishing, camping, or just about anything to do with outdoor adventures has a tendency to result in competition. Maybe it has something to do with our primitive instinct for survival, because there was a point in time when competition had serious implications. You either came out ahead, or you might not continue to exist.

Things have improved a lot since then. Winning doesn't necessarily mean you get to survive, but losing doesn't mean that your demise is at hand either. At least not usually. Winning does mean you get to gloat a little, or a lot. Losing means you get to listen to the winner. That may cause the loser to wish the end had come.

Camping probably has the least amount of risk associated with its competition as compared to other outdoor activities. However, there can be competitive camping. One competitive camping event is campfire cooking. However, campfire cooking competition can only begin after the campfire building competition has ended.

Campfire building starts with finding someone that is willing to round up firewood. Good firewood is hard for some people to find. I've noticed that experienced campers usually have a terrible time finding firewood. It seems that each successive time someone is sent for firewood, it becomes more difficult for them to find anything suitable for burning. They also have a tendency to complain more each time they are sent.

It is good to take a new person along on each camping trip. A new person is usually the best person to send for firewood. A simple explanation about bringing back only dry wood has miraculous results. The new person will be back inside of ten minutes with enough firewood to build the campfires for three days. Someone that has been sent for firewood a few times in the past will come back in thirty minutes and ask for a crew to go along and help find some wood.

After firewood is brought to the campsite, it is time to start the campfire building competition. The cook is usually expected to start the competition by picking up the first piece of wood. At that point everyone has a chance to be the champion fire builder. Nobody but the cook must touch the wood, but everyone is permitted to give instructions on how to stack the wood for the best burn.

It is sometimes difficult to reach a final decision as to who the winner is. Many times the winner will identify himself. It might be done in a rather casual manner, such as through a simple statement. "The food would have been much better cooked over a fire with the firewood sloping to the east as I earlier told you to do."

If the cook or bystander gets singed or burned, someone is immediately eliminated from the competition for contributing to a fire that could result in injury. The elimination notice goes something like this: "You *!#*, you caused the wood to be placed on the fire where it would cause the flame to be too hot."

After the fire building competition has eased up a bit, and the fire has died down to a level that it can be used for cooking, the first phase of the cooking competition can begin. Cooking competition goes through several stages. You can't really be sure when cooking competition is completed. It may appear to be over after the completion of a meal, only to surface again the next time a meal is to be cooked. The cooking competition in some camping groups carries over from one trip to another.

It starts with someone being assigned to do the cooking. Making a cooking assignment is necessary because it isn't wise to take a volunteer cook on a camping trip. Volunteer cooks are usually the worst. When a cook is appointed, he gets to cook the meal with very little help — but plenty of people watch. Cooks can't be trusted.

Camping rules permit the cook to assign dish washing to the first person who complains about the food. Sometimes the cooks have an incentive to do something to the food to bring out a complaint. That is why everyone keeps an eye on the cook.

The competitive aspect of cooking is for the cook to see if a position can be assumed that blocks everyone's view of the food. If this can be accomplished, one of the hamburgers or hotdogs can be altered to bring a complaint from its recipient. Completing an alteration of the food without being detected makes the cook the winner.

Several other camping competitions exist, but it will take too long to tell about all of them. Telling them would also require explanations that may give away my competitive edge when I am on a campout with my kids. Areas in which I still enjoy a competitive time with my family are: tent erection, tent take down, packing the car, camp cot selection, air mattress inflation, and port-a-potty cleaning. You can figure out your own rules for most of these.

Everyone that ever wet a hook knows about fishing competition. In my opinion, fishing competition has gone too far. Bass fishermen now pay to enter tournaments to see who can catch the most fish in a day or two. They even hire impartial judges to verify who has really won.

I think fishing competition was much better when it was left to the anglers to determine who had won, and the only prize was bragging rights. The bragging rights were only good until someone beat the current record between those in the competitive group. Depending on the group rules, which were never written, the competition might start new each fishing season.

Informal competition can become fierce, yet friendly. Ben Hooker is a friend of mine that has a competitive spirit that won't quit. He has a fishing spot that he won't tell anyone about, except to describe the fish he catches there. Each spring Ben tells of catching two and three pound crappie in his fishing spot. I can't seem to find a place with crappie bigger than twelve ounces, so I keep losing the crappie competition to Ben.

I tend to win the bluegill competition. I have learned to let Ben come back from a bluegill fishing trip and describe his catch before I ever go fishing. Once Ben has caught his bluegill and reported his results, I know how big of fish I must catch. It is a simple process to win the bluegill competition at this point. I only catch bluegill that in my eyes appear bigger than what Ben described.

Informal competition never requires the use of a tape measure or scale. Anyone willing to enter an informal competition must also be willing to trust everyone's ability as a wildlife estimator. Most informal competitors are willing to guess a fish's weight to within 3 ounces and its length to within one half inch. Small fish, under two pounds, may be guessed within an ounce. These abilities can develop early in life. Even a boy of five years can usually estimate the length of his fish when reporting his fishing successes. My grandson had no trouble at all after we released that first bluegill. When asked, without hesitation he held his hands up to show me the length of his fish. That boy will win a lot of competitions.

Anyone can be a winner of an informal fishing competition. It is almost as if the fishing did not matter. It is only necessary to understand the group rules, and learn to abide by them. The rules are pretty simple and sometimes they develop as unwritten and unstated rules. As an example, I never ask Ben where his crappie fishing hole is, nor do I ask if he has put any of his big crappie on a scale. Just as Ben always tells me about his bluegill fishing trips before I have had a chance to go fishing, I tell him about my crappie fishing trip before he goes. So far, he has always won the crappie fishing contest, and I have always won the bluegill contest.

Ben and I have another friend who is a bass fisherman. He hardly ever fishes for crappie or bluegill. I guess that explains why he catches so many large bass. Every year he reports bass catches that make me envious. He has even taken me along a few times, and I always had really high expectations. Oddly, the big bass never hit on the days he took me along. We consistently catch bass that are between twelve ounces and one pound six ounces.

These small bass look a lot like the ones caught by the professional fishermen on TV. Of course the TV is a strange apparatus. It causes fish to appear smaller than they really are. I guess it is the camera angle. Each time a bass is pulled out of the water, I estimate the weight of the fish. Shortly afterward, the guy on TV guesses a weight that is at least one or two pounds heavier than my guess.

Competition certainly is not limited to camping and fishing. Hunters and people in contact with them know about the hunting competition, but the seriousness of the competition may vary among the occasional and the hard core hunters. Until recently, hunting competition was left to the amateurs who hunt for sport and food. Professional competition in hunting is a relatively new activity and I sincerely hope that professional hunting tournaments are not allowed to persist. That will be the ruin of hunting for people that enjoy the sport as amateurs.

Amateur hunting competition is an interesting thing to witness. It may not seem very organized to a non-hunter, but to those of us who have hunted over many years, it is a ritual. Everyone is in the competition whether they know it or not. The rules are somewhat fluid so long as nobody violates the federal or state wildlife code. Although hunting competition may sometimes look a little ruthless to the newcomer, all responsible sportsmen understand the importance of compliance with all laws. Failure to do so not only puts the violator at risk of arrest, but it also can result in banishment from all future competition with fellow sportsmen.

So, am I off base or is there really an undocumented competition between complete strangers within the hunting world? Let me ask this. What are the first words from one hunter to another after deer season is over? Are they not, "Did you get one?" The only hunter that does not greet you with these words is a hunter that didn't fill his tag. Oh, someone may disguise the question to avoid being too obvious. It could sound something like, "How did your deer hunt go?"

The way in which the greeting is made can tell you a lot about how well the hunter asking the question did on his hunt. Little signals can indicate that this guy bagged the biggest deer in the state, or that he shot a yearling that should still be in the field.

Regardless of that, the utterance of the greeting is a sure sign that the judging of the hunt is about to begin. It may even be a proclamation of victory, or a signal of surrender.

A response to the greeting can be just as full of information as the greeting itself. A simple, but confident, "Ya, I got one," means a fairly good size deer was harvested. A simple, but quiet, "Ya, I got a small one for eating this year," means a yearling doe was taken. Nobody ever shoots a small deer except to get some tender meat for eating. Once in a while you get a pathetic, "No, all I saw were small and I let them go." A person saying this may have a lot to hide, and they should be thoroughly questioned to determine just what happened. Watch for fidgeting and shifting eyes or maybe a nervous rubbing of one arm. Finally, there is the pathetic, "Man, I sure hope you did better than me." The words may not reflect what he is really thinking.

The size of the animal is not the only factor in determining the winner of the competition. The difficulty of the shot is just as important. I've made a couple of shots that my listeners found difficult to believe. Having a witness to a story is important if a difficult shot is to be used as part of the claims made. This takes a good hunting buddy, and an agreement to back up each other's stories. If done correctly, two buddies working together can emerge in a tie for the championship of that year.

The deer championship is a difficult competition to judge. As time goes on, each hunter remembers a little more. These periodic memory improvements can result in some changes in who is leading in the competition. It is considered poor form to have two memory improvements in the same day.

The more often a story is told by a hunter, the more they remember, and the more fantastic their shot becomes. After thinking about this a little, I believe everyone should be a hunter. It would significantly improve the collective memory of our country.

My friend Windy was an archer and a hunter. Windy and I worked together, so we had plenty of opportunity to hear one another tell stories. When those stories were about things we did together, I sometimes winced when I heard his versions begin to include actions by Windy that I had no recall of having seen. He may have responded similarly as one of my stories began.

Now, it isn't to be said by me that the things in his stories never happened, because he once quietly told me that he was having difficulty remembering some of the things I had done. From his comment I came to realize that I may not remember his actions as well as he can.

His self-restraint and appreciation for my attempts to remember things with the correct level of detail is a good sign of friendship and I feel obligated to respond in kind. So, it appears that one hunter can have a memory improvement when others in the hunting party don't have a similar improvement. Such is life, and among hunting buddies such things are understood to be completely normal.

Windy and I archery hunted for gar in the local rivers, and one year we decided to deer hunt together. Now, I'll freely admit that he was a better archer than me. In fact, he was as good of an archery shot as I knew, and he did not need to embellish his stories regarding his abilities, but that really did not deter him.

Our deer stands were 247 yards apart. I was in a blind on the ground, and he was in a tree. On the very first morning, before 7:00 a.m., he was successful in harvesting a state record size whitetail buck. The weight of the deer and the size of the antlers placed the deer in the top ten in the state.

Amazing as the size of the deer was, the improvement in Windy's memory of events experienced during the deer hunt were phenomenal. At first, the shot was a little better than the average archer should try. As time went on, more detail was remembered about the hunt, and the shot itself became an ultimate archery experience. The story as I first heard it was a once in a lifetime event, but when Windy completed his memory recovery, the story was something fitting for the Hunt Of A Lifetime series on the Outdoor Adventures television network.

Immediately after the successful shot, Windy didn't quite remember just how things had happened. I suppose all the excitement caused him some confusion, which he was able to sort out as time passed. His initial confusion caused him to omit important details and get a few facts distorted. Fortunately, his story was perfected as he reached what appeared to be a 100% memory recovery.

The following versions of the story that morphed over time show just how this phenomenon can unfold. I've inserted my comments in brackets. This is only one example of the very common memory recovery that can occur among hunters, fishermen, and all people that experience outdoor adventures.

One hour after the shot:

The deer came out of the woods about sixty yards away. He was moseying through the open field. When he was broadsided to me at about thirty yards, I pulled back, focused on the appropriate spot, and let the arrow fly. It went into the left shoulder, and he took off like all get out [all get out is really fast and with excellent agility]. When he crossed the little creek down at the end of the field, another hunter saw where it went. The guy was decent and realized I had put a good hit on him. He pointed out where my deer was last seen. After I field dressed it, the guy helped me drag it out.

One day later:

The deer emerged from the woods about sixty yards away. He was really moving [the deer's correct speed was recalled]. When he was broadsided to me at about forty yards [better recollection of distance], I let the arrow fly. It went in just behind the left shoulder [remembered more precisely the arrow placement]. The deer was struggling to continue, but he somehow managed to get across the creek [recalled the effects of the mortal wound]. There was a guy down there that helped me drag him out [reduction of the distraction caused by too many details about another hunter].

One week later:

This monster whitetail buck with a record size rack [added reference to record size] came out of the woods about sixty yards away. He was almost in a run [better terminology applied to communicate speed and clarify the difficulty of shot]. When he was broadsided to me at about fifty yards [final mental reconstruction of scene and appropriate adjustment of distance], I let the arrow fly. It went in just behind the left shoulder and went cleanly through the heart [added previously omitted specific vital organ hit]. His momentum must have enabled him to make it to the creek [clearer illustration of the effect of the hit], because he was mortally wounded as soon as the arrow left the string. It was a real struggle dragging him to the truck [elimination of the distraction of another hunter in the story].

Final Version:

I'll not repeat the perfectly reconstructed story, but in the final and most accurately remembered version of the facts, the utilized hunting skills and the vast size of the deer were clearly portrayed without any need for distracting details of others that were in the field that day. I was not directly involved in any part of the story until the deer was in the truck, so I was fine with the fact that my presence was only noted as a witness to the full truth. When my role is that of witness, I've learned it is best not to help a hunting buddy with his memory corrections. Hunters and all outdoorsmen are quite capable of getting their own stories perfected.

This last and most accurate version of what became known as The Big Deer Story was shared widely with coworkers, friends, family, the archery community, and anyone that happened by at a good time to talk. I was fortunate to hear Windy's story dozens of times, and of course simply nodded my head in agreement. The primary facts remained consistent, and the memory recovery handled the periphery details in an interesting way that made the story fun to hear and easy to agree with.

Abiding by the spirit of competition and unwritten rules will help to maintain friendships among hunters and fishermen even when one has what is considered a "significant" memory recovery. Windy and I remain friends.

I never came close to harvesting a deer that would have beat the one that Windy took home. He won the deer hunting contest that year regardless of any memory improvement that took place. There was of course something that kept my hopes up. There would be another season in the future and another chance to beat him.

From the stories shared above, the dynamic of friendly competition can to some extent be understood, and perhaps some guidance for effective competition can be found in the stories. Here's one item to be considered when conducting competition.

Understand that for the best chance of winning a friendly competition, the judging should always be completed as soon as possible after an event. Any judgments made at the end of a trip should be final. Reconsideration should not be permitted. Should reconsideration be mistakenly permitted, it will result in all the people in the competition having memory improvements, and the last one to talk will probably have the largest improvement of all and end up the winner.

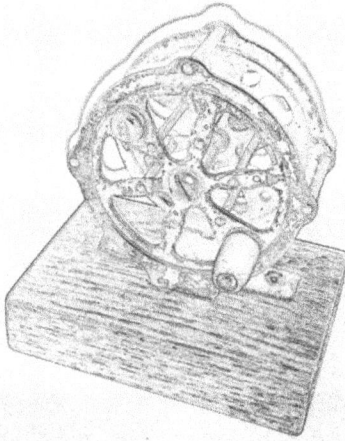

Fly Casting Reel

RODS AND REELS

Rod and reel selection these days can cause a lot of confusion for anyone that learned to fish more than ten years ago. I feel like I've stepped into some imaginary futuristic world when I walk into a large sporting goods store. It's sort of like waiting ten years between trips to the electronics store. You're apt to be looking for a knob to turn on the TV, and what it really takes is a six year old punching a key sequence on a hand held control.

I grew up in the emerging electronics age, so I don't have any problem turning on my TV. Well that's not completely true if I want to switch from the satellite to the DVD player. I need the instruction manual for that. However, regardless of the changes in TVs, I'm having trouble figuring out the modern day fishing equipment and the new terminology that is being used.

Most of my fishing equipment is more than ten years old. Actually, some of it was my father's and is probably more than forty years old. The thing is, I still know how to operate it. There have been times when purchasing a new rod or casting reel was on my mind, but I couldn't figure out what to buy.

Regardless of the challenges previously encountered trying to buy modern fishing equipment, I have at various times decided that I need something new. Being a creature of habit, I would make a trip to Peak's Sporting Goods in my hometown if Mr. Peak was still there. Mr. Peak's store was where I bought much of my stuff as a boy and young man. Mr. Peak would always help me find something that met my needs and my budget.

I'm sure he had fond memories of me and appreciated the fact that I made many of the payments on his home. Assuming that someone else now runs his store, they probably would not recognize me as I haven't been around for quite some time. If Mr. Peak told them about me, I'm sure they would be glad to have me make a visit.

Mr. Peak always knew that when I walked in, there was pretty much a sure sale. He liked me. No wasted time, just a simple sale. Usually, he would end up with most of the money I had with me except, he would leave enough for me to buy a bottle of soda at Mamie's Sweet Shop down the street. When I was a kid, a soda only required a dime. As a young man, it was about fifty cents. Today, it is probably two dollars.

As I recently contemplated a possible trip to Peak's Sporting Goods store, I did a little browsing through the latest Big Bluegill catalog. Now I'm confused.

I turned to the RODS section of the catalog, expecting it to be about three pages long. One page was for casting rods, one for spinning rods, and one for fly rods. I thought there might be a fourth page for fiberglass fishing poles. It's a side thought, but I still don't understand why fiberglass poles were allowed to replace cane poles. I happily used cane poles for my first twenty years of bluegill and crappie fishing.

There are 53 pages of rods. What a surprise!

It took several minutes to locate what I thought looked like a casting rod. It was called a flippin' stick. It costs $78. My brother and I would cut a free flippin' stick from a willow tree when we were kids. Stick a firecracker on the end of it and you could flip it twenty or thirty feet in the air. Don't know why I would want to pay $78 for something that I can cut from a willow tree.

I never did find anything called a casting rod. Several items looked like casting rods, but were called something else. I guess

I could buy one of those other things and use it for a casting rod if I want to. Fishing sure is getting complicated.

Fishing was fun when it was simple. My father taught me simple methods that usually work. We always caught fish unless something went wrong with the barometer, or the wind switched to come out of the east.

Our simple methods were not expensive. Bluegill fishing called for a cane pole, a piece of fishing line about the length of the pole, a leader about fifteen inches long, and a #4 hook. The sinker was a small piece of lead hammered into a thin strip. Wrap a piece of thin lead around your leader and squeeze it in place, and you have an adjustable sinker that can be removed to use on another line. A lot of people use lead shot because they don't realize that a strip of lead is much easier to adjust, or remove. Let's see you remove a piece of split shot from your line after it was squeezed on with a pair of pliers.

Our corks were small bottle stoppers. These are far better than plastic bobbers. Bottle stoppers do not make a splash that scares away half the fish in the lake.

Place a gob of worms on the hook, and bluegill can actually be caught with this simple setup. Crickets or small crawfish can also be used. A crawfish of the right size is hard to beat. Cockroaches are good, but if you use this particular bait you are going to find that it is hard to keep them at home. Spouses seem to get upset about cockroaches.

The cane pole was a special piece of equipment. Each year required a new one. Cane poles tend to dry out over time. They bend a lot better while they are still green. They could be bought from any country store. Store owners had a neat way of tying them in a bundle that stood on end. The bundle was placed in plain sight of anyone going down the road.

It was a simple matter to pull in and stop at the store, select a pole, pay a dollar for it, and be on your way. These poles didn't have a joint in them, so it was necessary to travel with them in the boat or with the back window down if hauling them in the car. The poles were inserted through the back window with the big end resting on the front floorboard of the car. The small end would be left to protrude outside. It didn't look odd. Everyone going fishing had the same kind of setup.

My father, brother, and I could select our poles in about five minutes. In that amount of time I could pick up all the poles in the bundle and whip them through the air to test their flexibility. Testing one pole at a time was acceptable, but it showed better dexterity to test a pole in each hand. Store owners love to see a kid do this. It gives them a chance to show their agility as they dodge the ends of the poles.

I doubt the cane pole will ever make a comeback, but if it does, I will celebrate. Meantime, I will continue to use the fiberglass pole that I purchased in 1973. It still works fine, there is no need to buy another one. That's too bad. My children and grandchildren have missed out on the experience of stopping to try out cane poles each spring.

Now that I think about it, I wonder if the store owners had anything to do with the demise of the cane pole.

If I decide to buy a new fishing rod, I might as well get a new reel, too. From the Big Bluegill catalog that I have, it appears that every fisherman in the state could have a unique reel. I have no idea why there are so many types of reels. Some of them are advertised to be good for palming. That is confusing for sure. Palming isn't even a fishing term if I'm right. I thought it was a basketball term that means you didn't dribble the ball correctly, and the other team gets to have the ball.

Reel prices range from about $40 to waaaayyy over $100. I can't tell what is different about these reels by reading the words in the catalog. Am I supposed to be smart enough to already know what the difference is? Or should I trust the manufacturer to have prices that reflect the quality of each item? How does a person know what amount of money it takes to obtain the quality level and functions desired for the type and amount of fishing to be done?

Perhaps some fishermen need a selection of reels as big as is offered in the Big Bluegill catalog, but I can't imagine why. I can't even figure out the differences between them.

Perhaps the best thing to do is just go somewhere like Peak's Sporting Goods store and see what the people there say. Maybe they know what all this stuff is good for.

Complicating the selection of poles, rods and reels is enough to frustrate me, but the things that have been done to fishing bait have me confused. It is true that artificial bait has been around for a long time. Real bait has been around longer. I'm not sure why most people use artificial bait. Perhaps it is because real bait is hard to catch these days. Surely it has nothing to do with the fact that real bait is a little nasty.

Have you felt or smelled the stuff that people spray on artificial bait. It is the oiliest, smelliest fluid in the universe. I have never held a piece of live bait that smelled so bad, or would cause your boat bottom to be so slippery. Anyone that uses this stuff can't possibly have anything against real bait.

Live bait is hard to find. Someone found a way to stake a claim on all the live bait in the country, and charge outrageous prices for it. Last year I paid 10% of a week's income just to get some worms. When I opened them up, the reason for the high price was obvious. They had sold me all the baby worms. Finding worms this small must have been a real chore and deserved more money for all the effort.

Live bait was always caught by the person that planned to use it when I was a kid. A few exceptions existed, but we country people always did find city people a little strange.

We caught crawfish out of a pond. A farmer we knew had a pond that was the crawfish breeding capital of the Midwest. We seined small crawfish in the spring for bluegill fishing. Through June and July we got larger ones for trotline fishing. Even though we took several hundred at a time, we were careful to put the breeding stock back in the pond. It worked for years. The farmer was always happy to see us, because we took him a mess of fish each time we went. The barter system was alive and working. As luck would have it, our bait pond is now in the middle of Rend Lake. The army corps of engineers probably knew that my family actually had one good thing going and purposefully built the lake to wipe out our good fortune. I've never found another bait hole like that one.

When I was a kid, people who bought worms from a store were sending a loud message regarding their sporting knowledge. They obviously didn't know much. We always had plenty of big lively worms. We grew them in our garden. Coffee grounds and leftovers buried in the garden on a daily basis seemed to be adequate to keep a healthy supply of worms available.

Things do change. Cane poles were replaced by fiberglass. Casting and spinning rods are now replaced by flippin' sticks and other such funny named items. Reels turn into palming devices with digital readout computers. But one thing doesn't change. Regardless of your fishing equipment, fish would rather eat a live bug or crustacean than a piece of plastic smeared with smelly goop.

Try it, they'll like it.

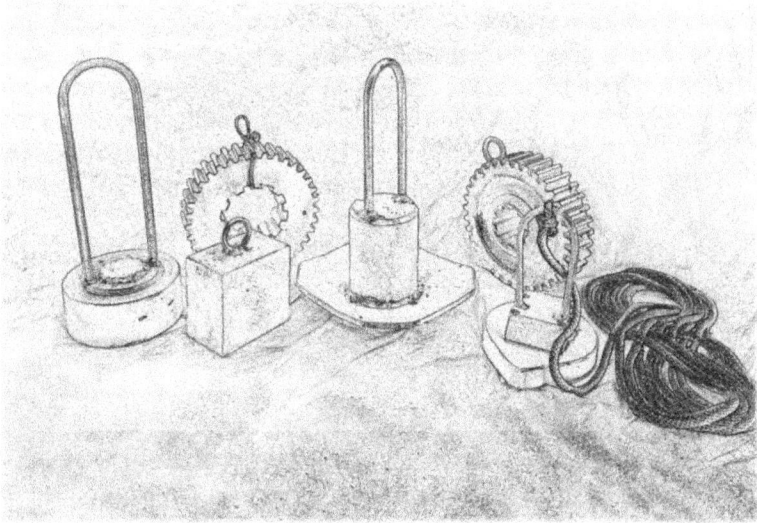

Homemade Anchors

ANCHORS AWAY

Fishermen know that an anchor is an essential piece of equipment. I can't overstress how important it is to possess the right anchor for a boat or a trotline. Boat owners that do not fish probably know the importance of having a good anchor, but it is only a trotline fisherman that holds a truly high appreciation for a really good anchor, one that is capable of holding a trotline. I'm a trotline fisherman, or at least I've been one.

Growing up fishing trotlines in the Ohio River gave me an understanding of the importance of a good anchor. For the inexperienced I will try to briefly explain, but this may be hard to understand, because only the tried and true fishermen develop special feelings toward their anchors. To lose one before its time is an emotional event. Seldom will a fisherman experience a greater equipment loss than to have a good anchor disappear before it is ready to be retired.

In my experience, it was uncommon to come across a good anchor by accident. Obtaining good anchors required fabricating them from raw material, or making a careful selection from among the myriad of mediocre weights that exist in the boating world. A store bought anchor was seldom going to exactly meet the need, and it would probably cost far too much.

The anchor selection process could be learned in any of several ways. I learned through a combination of tutorial experiences and trial-and-error. The lessons learned by trial-and-error have stayed with me real well because this methodology has a way of making lessons stick.

Anchor selection was something that had to be done with an understanding of what the anchor was to do. First and foremost, it must hold something in a desired location in a body of water. That's it. Now, there are additional criteria that shouldn't be overlooked.

An anchor must be shaped appropriately and of adequate weight to do the job. It should be light enough that it may be raised and placed back in the boat. Anchor utilization is another matter, and that includes such things as securing the anchor to the item that will be anchored, appropriately dropping anchor, and of course, retrieving the anchor. This utilization of anchors will be touched upon a little later.

Let's first deal with the criteria that an anchor must be the correct weight. Shape is important, but weight is the primary concern for a fisherman. A light anchor makes retrieval easier than if using a heavy one, and it is acceptable to use a light anchor if the thing you attach to the anchor doesn't drift away. If your anchored item is gone when you attempt to retrieve it, the anchor was too light. For those that are having trouble following along, pick a heavier anchor the next time.

A heavy anchor is more likely to hold a secured item in place, but an anchor that is too heavy can be difficult to lift without a winch. If a person opts for extra-heavy anchors and a winch, I suggest being careful about who you tell that you fish with a winch. They may not know the difference between a winch and a wench. It could get you in trouble at home.

My first lessons regarding anchor selection were given to me at the age of ten. My father fished trotlines in the Ohio River with great success. He learned from a commercial fisherman during the Great Depression. Because my father once earned his living from the fish he caught, he took the anchor selection process seriously. He attempted to pass the selection knowledge to my brother and me. The initial lessons he taught us were related to selecting expendable anchors for trotlines.

Now, not every word that my father spoke was heard, and not all that was heard was always understood. Of the things heard and understood, only some of it was sufficiently committed to memory to ensure its proper application in the future. So, there may be some of my own invention in the things that I do. Moving along, I'll continue to explain about my learning experiences in anchor selection.

Sometimes, I would get distracted by something such as an attack dragonfly while Dad was telling me how to select an anchor or tie a trotline to an anchor. He might not notice that I had been under attack as he continued to teach, and therefore he would not know that I only heard part of what he said. I also assumed that I had heard everything that mattered.

For trotlines, we typically did not use fabricated weights for our anchors. We had a ready-made stockpile of well-shaped rocks along a bluff on one shore of the Ohio River. One time, we were selecting anchors, just downstream from Rosiclare, Illinois. Dad was explaining how to properly pick up a rock to avoid getting bitten by a snake that might be lying beneath it. He had previously given us enough lessons about the local copperheads and rattlesnakes so that we all knew to be cautious.

In the middle of his explanation about properly turning over rocks, I experienced a ferocious dragonfly attack. Such an attack could result in some quick movement such as ducking and flailing of arms. As a result, I only heard part of what he said. I heard him say "be careful ... (dragonfly attack) ... to keep the snake from biting you." He had no way of knowing why I had abruptly abandoned the hunt for anchors and was leaping up and down as I departed the area. I was rapidly making my way back to the boat, and I heard him shout a warning of something about not running on a rock pile because that could break an ankle. I was in the boat before I asked where the snake went. He just kind of shook his head. He sometimes did that after explaining things to me.

Anchors were selected very carefully from the rock pile. A rectangular shape was ideal. It would stay flat on the river bottom, and it was easy to tie a trotline onto it. This tying of the trotline was a key part of correctly using an anchor. Believe me, if the trotline is not tied to the anchor, it will not help at all. Pay attention to the previous bit of information. This one is important.

Regarding the shape of our trotline anchors, round rocks were of little or no help, because they rolled on the river bottom. Rectangular was a firm requirement.

The size of our anchors was determined according to the time of year and how fast the river was running. To me, the rocks seemed big during autumn when the river was barely moving. In the spring, we used mammoth size anchors. My anchor size judgments were based upon my ability to lift them when they were tied to the main staging of a trotline. Big anchors only caused the string to hurt my hands a little bit. Mammoth size anchors caused the string to slip through my fingers and leave red whelps.

Before I go forward, I'll explain that my father was generally a kind and patient man. But he did have his limits, and he also had some expectations of fellow fishermen, regardless of age.

There seemed to be other factors that sometimes influenced the size of anchors my father selected. One of those factors was sometimes, but not always, who fished with us. I noticed a correlation between people fishing with us that didn't do much work around the camp, and the trips when Dad selected larger than normal anchors. The morning the trotlines were pulled out of the water, the special guests were given the privilege of retrieving one of the trotlines that was well anchored. If they returned for another trip, one size larger may be required. This process could be repeated as needed.

Boat anchors are a lot different than trotline anchors. No self-respecting fisherman would ever put a rock on the end of a rope for a boat anchor. However, I have seen some fisherman fill a milk jug with concrete and use it for an anchor, but this too is a little on the tacky side.

Boat shops sell some neat looking anchors for the less fortunate fishermen who don't have the resources available to make a real boat anchor. Real boat anchors are made from steel. A welder friend or machinist can usually make a boat anchor that a person can be proud of.

The bottom of the anchor can be made from one inch thick steel plate cut in an oval or a modified heart shape. Let's call it a triangle with rounded corners. Don't use an unmodified heart shape, like from a valentine, unless you want to be laughed off the river or lake.

On top of the base plate, weld a four or five inch cube of steel. Then, make a loop or a large letter U shape of 1/4 inch diameter steel rod. Make the letter U perhaps five inches high. Seven or eight inches high would be even better. Weld the U shape to the top of the steel cube to serve as a tie point. That loop should be tall enough that the anchor topples over to let the anchor bottom 'bite' into the lake or river bottom. This kind of anchor was adequate for a twelve or fourteen foot aluminum fishing boat on a small body of water where there was only a light breeze or slow current. Scale up the size of the anchor for larger boats, higher wind conditions, and rivers with a substantial current.

If care was taken to avoid selecting an undersized anchor for a boat, it could become a multipurpose piece of equipment. A large anchor could be used for ballast when only one person was in the boat if the boat didn't seem to be sitting correctly on the water. If really heavy, it was best not to place two of those anchors at one end or at one side of the boat.

After giving it a little more thought, anchors can become multipurpose regardless of their size. My family has experienced times when we ran out of trotline anchors and had to resort to using our boat anchors on the trotlines. Such resourcefulness can be evidence of the dedication and resourcefulness of the fisherman. It can be impressive to those who do not ordinarily face such difficult hardships on a daily basis.

On one of our family fishing trips, I had the need to use not only one of my boat anchors as a trotline weight, but I had to use the front and rear anchors. Such a condition could appear as forgetfulness for not having brought enough trotline anchors, but in reality it was not. I pondered on the question of what could have caused me to come up short on the number or trotline anchors, and the only possible reason that came to mind was that I became distracted by all the additional preparation required to go fishing with inexperienced helpers.

This particular event took place while trotline fishing in the Rock River near Sterling, Illinois. The problem was connected in some way to the fact that I took my wife and daughter with me to put the trotlines in the river. Keep in mind that I had fished trotlines from the time I was a small boy, and I had developed an expertise that was only overshadowed by that of my father.

One of the things that I learned growing up as a fisherman was that risks exist anytime a person attempts to fish with the inexperienced. Every fisherman knows that taking along inexperienced people can cause almost painful levels of forgetfulness, distraction, and unexplainable foibles. Yet we take them along because they are friends or family, and we want them to experience the fun of fishing. We might even be teaching them the art.

I was able to resist forgetfulness to a great extent on that outing to the Rock River, but one of the needed trotline anchors was left at home. I'll point out that by this time in my life, I was using home fabricated trotline anchors made of chunks of steel or large gears with a large lock washer welded to it. I placed several of them in the boat before leaving home, but I either miscounted or someone took one back out of the boat. It would not be immediately noticed that I was short on anchors because I was so busy doing things that an experienced helper normally did. This too would turn out okay, because a shortage of trotline anchors would let me demonstrate to Nellie and Sam just how resourceful I could be. It would be good for them, and it would help in their preparation for the day when they forget one of their trotline anchors.

I was preparing to put the last trotline in the river when I realized the anchor count was inadequate. Both of my inexperienced helpers denied removing the missing anchor, so I announced that it was fine because the situation allowed me to give a lesson on resourcefulness. A missing trotline anchor was no real problem. I had plenty of boat anchors with me. I would untie one from the boat and use it for the trotline. In only a few moments, I had the anchor untied from the boat. I moved the anchor to the back of the boat to be near the trotline. Nellie and Sam were both impressed. Of course, their expressions of amazement distracted me at the time when I was planning to tie the trotline to the anchor. Remember what I said earlier? An anchor does no good unless it is tied to the trotline.

While putting a trotline out, there is an ideal time for dropping the first anchor. As I recall the events, there was a feeling that a mistake was about to be made. I had this feeling well before it was a certainty. There was no time to worry about things that had not taken place. So, I positioned the boat and was lined up to put out the trotline.

I picked up the anchor and with the appropriate motion I tossed it. My fingers were straightened and the anchor was sliding off my fingertips. In a flash, I realized the trotline was not tied to the anchor. If only there was a pause button. It made the familiar arc through the air that normally gets the trotline started out of the jumper box, and then it splashed into the water. Well, boat anchor number one was lost.

It took a few seconds to realize who had caused it. There was no point in telling my wife and daughter that they were to blame. I felt bad for them, because surely they realized their part in causing this terrible loss to happen. I was experiencing feelings of pity for them because I for a moment thought they would have trouble coping with their feelings of guilt.

I turned to look. Nellie and Sam had looks of amazement on their faces. Their eyes were wide open, their lips pressed together, even their backs were straight and stiff. This was the first of a series of expressions that reflected the various emotions they used to cover their feelings of guilt. Their looks of amazement changed to smiles as the ends of their lips began to curve upwards, then their teeth exposed and eyes squinted some, then laughter. It was obvious from the emotional display of expressions that they were working hard to cover up their feeling a great burden of guilt. I knew they fully realized the impact of what they had caused. Otherwise, they wouldn't have worked so hard at covering up their true feelings. I'd seen this behavior from them before. Rather than cope with their guilt feelings, they made what I saw as a feeble attempt to mask their suppressed emotions with laughter.

Even though I said nothing, it was only a few seconds before they collected their thoughts and began to deny any guilt. As unimaginable as it may seem, they began to blame me for the whole series of events. They've stuck to that process of shifting blame for a long time. Some of the stories they passed on to others gave me the impression that they were thrilled to have been out fishing with me, and thoroughly delighted to have an embarrassing moment to bring up at any moment in my future. They would never come to admit they had distracted me and caused this terrible event.

The loss of just any anchor wouldn't be too upsetting. I could even deal with the fact that we had passed the ideal location for the trotline to be put out. What really bothered me was that my favorite anchor was now at the river bottom. Fishing couldn't possibly be the same without my favorite anchor. I still miss that anchor.

One positive lesson did come from this event. I was able to demonstrate the importance of being doubly resourceful. Another boat anchor was still in the boat. I untied it. Everyone was told to stop laughing while I showed them the correct way to secure a trotline to an anchor. After inspecting the knot a few times, it was thrown out, and this time the trotline was successfully put in the water.

After teaching people a lesson about resourcefulness, it is amazing how much can be remembered about the lesson and surrounding events. I have total recall of this particular fishing trip, especially the loss of my favorite anchor. It's as though things moved in slow motion, giving me time to see everything.

I must say they have said far less than I thought they would. They have only mentioned this event four or five times. Key times when the right people were present and it could be a major blow to the perception others have of my outstanding fishing knowledge and ability. They have always failed to mention their contribution to the loss of my favorite anchor.

It hasn't bothered me very much.

Potential Hunting Paradise

HUNTING PLACES

Finding a place to hunt was a fairly simple thing to do when I was a kid. We departed from our house a few minutes early on days we weren't going to one of our regular hunting locations. The extra few minutes allowed us time to stop and ask permission from the owner of a new hunting place. Dad would drive up to the nearest farmhouse by a likely looking hunting spot, go knock on the door, and ask for permission. Usually, the farmer would look dad over, glance at the car to see that he had two upstanding young sons, and then extend his permission for us to hunt.

More often than not, the farmer provided detailed information about property lines, neighbors that wouldn't mind us hunting, and where the most rabbits normally held up. Things changed. Some call it progress.

Over the last forty or fifty years, so much has changed that attitudes were affected. Of course, farmers always had the right to control who went on their property. That is the way it should be. Unfortunately, the changes in the world gave farmers cause to be more cautious about letting people hunt on their farms.

The results achieved by knocking on a farmer's door are different today than they were a few decades in the past. In fact, just finding the correct door to knock on is a challenge with many farms now owned by someone that does not live on or near it.

Having grown up in a small town during an era when farmers let people hunt, it is hard to tolerate conditions as they are today. Living near a city during these times makes it worse. It seems that nobody within thirty miles of a city lets anyone hunt, and beyond thirty miles, hunting is restricted to hunters that aren't from the city.

To ensure I have a place to hunt when season comes in, it is necessary to go out hunting places well in advance of the season when I plan to hunt game. Hunting places, and hunting on places are now two completely separate activities.

I am not really sure when the best time is for hunting places. The techniques for hunting places are also something of a puzzle. Several combinations of times and techniques have been investigated, all with such random results that no logical conclusions can be drawn.

Several unsuccessful attempts one summer resulted in my enlistment of a friend to give me some help. Willie was from a small town just the same as I was, and he understood the frustrations that I faced. Perhaps with the two of us pleading, some farmer might give us permission.

Prior to actually going out to look for a place, we made an agreement. Our agreement was that any hunting places we found would be shared. We would never take anyone else to the new places, but we could hunt it alone or together. This seemed to be a good deal because Willie worked a lot of overtime and wouldn't get to hunt very much.

We set aside a Saturday morning to go hunting places. Willie picked me up because he had the perfect vehicle for it. It was a three year old pickup truck, with air conditioning. Looking for a hunting place in August does require air conditioning. The age of the truck was also judged to be about right. It was old enough to be imperfect and not look like we held mountains of money that permitted us to buy new trucks every year. It was new enough not to look as if though we were two derelicts wanting to move in and take over. Willie chewed tobacco and I did not. We could alternate who did the talking depending on whether or not the farmer had a wad in his mouth.

My clothing was carefully selected. My blue jeans were well broken in, but not ragged. New blue jeans might give the impression I didn't often wear country clothing. Ragged jeans would give the appearance that I don't take care of things. They fit and would stay up where they belonged. I was attempting to dress appropriately for the task. Willie wasn't aware of the need to dress just right for the occasion. He had on good slacks like he wore to work, a shirt with a button down collar, and polished slippers. After thirty minutes of my adjusting and conditioning his clothing, we were ready to go. Rubbing medium grit sandpaper across the knees of his slacks made them appear to be well used. A few specks of paint on his shirt made it look old enough, and a little cleaning fluid took the shine right off his shoes. It was difficult to get all this done in a half hour with Willie complaining and jumping around all the time.

Finally, we headed off to start hunting places. We drove about fifteen miles, and turned down a gravel road. Our maps of the area gave us some clues as to where to start. It wasn't long until we saw a good looking farm. My wildlife estimating experience was immediately put into action, and that resulted in an estimate that this place should have a lot of deer on it.

The farm house sat a ways up a little dirt lane. As we approached, we began to discuss who should actually initiate the inquiry. Willie wasn't as experienced as me, so I lost the argument when he insisted that the person with the most experience should start off the conversation.

The house was showing some signs of wear. I was fairly pleased that I wasn't overdressed. Also the car in the driveway didn't look real good. Perhaps with a little luck this guy would identify with us and be willing to let us hunt.

After knocking a few times, there was movement in the house, and a young man eventually opened the door. He looked a little sleepy, and asked what I wanted.

"Just out driving around with my good trustworthy friend and thought we would stop off to ask about hunting in this area."

The reaction was one that I didn't recognize. He grinned and shook his head in a way that wasn't a yes or a no. There was still hope. At least, up to this point, he had not refused. Perhaps there was still time to make acquaintances and convince him that Willie and I were safe, trustworthy, and respectful hunters. Perhaps I could put him in a good mood.

"Say, this weather has really turned off hot hasn't it."

Yes it had. Without air conditioning in his house, it had been so hot that it was hard to get to sleep after getting off work from the third shift. Perhaps he could soon get back to sleep this morning before it got too hot.

Seemed like a good time to change the subject. "I noticed your car over there as I came up the drive. It's a nice looking car. That white top and black sides is an interesting paint scheme."

It seems his car was all white, until yesterday. The road up the way had been oiled a couple of days ago. Even though his wife had been told to stay off the new oil and to use the other road, she decided to use the oiled road. As he explained what his wife did, he stopped using her name and began to use various terms when it was necessary to refer to her. Of course, by the time he had used some of those terms, she had sneakingly walked up beside him at the door. As he went on with his complaining about the car, I saw tears appear in her eyes, and then I heard words begin to flow from her mouth. What seemed like twenty minutes later, his eyes were extending two inches from their sockets, and he looked back at me and asked just what it was that I wanted?

Having listened to his concerns about the weather, his car, his wife, and now that I knew every misunderstanding between him and his wife, I was certain that he saw me as a friend of the family, or possibly as an adopted relative. The fact that I now knew everything his wife had done wrong for the past four years, it was logical that he would want me as a close friend to ensure I wasn't going around town telling stories. It was safe for me to now ask the question.

"Would you mind letting Willie and me do a little hunting when season comes in this year?"

A few seconds of silence went by. His eyes were back in their sockets and only one eyelid was twitching. He didn't know. He only rented the house.

We spent all that time becoming buddies with the wrong man, and he had more problems than a person could shake a stick at. The landowner lived in town. As far as our new friend knew, nobody had ever been permitted to hunt there.

After getting the owner's name and phone number, we went on down the road, hunting places.

The next place that we saw was a better looking wildlife haven than the first one. The farmhouse that sat on the property was one of those that caused me to feel a little uneasy. It had the old brown asphalt siding that was supposed to look like a brick pattern. The front porch was sagging, and nobody had used the front door in ten years. Usually, the front door not being used could be a good sign. People who use their back doors were usually friendly, but this time I wasn't certain. The big black Doberman Pinscher by the back door could negate all the other positive vibes coming from the unused front door.

There weren't any cars in the driveway. At least not any that moved in the last couple of years. This could mean that nobody was home, assuming they had a car that worked. But there was also a chance that someone was around, because the dog was running loose in the yard, and their Harley was in the yard.

The gate at the side of the driveway was latched, but not locked, so I suggested that Willie go and ask for permission. The upper lip on the Pinscher had curled some when I checked the gate latch. Willie was certain that nobody was home, but I insisted that he try. Besides, I had asked at the last place.

As Willie approached the gate, the dog stood up and walked toward the gate. He didn't growl or rough up his hackles. He just looked into Willie's eyes as he walked toward him. With Willie's hand on the gate, and the Doberman's nose two inches from his hand, Willie froze. He said something about not being sure what the dog intended to do. I assured him that the dog was only trying to smell him to make friends. Dogs make friends that way.

As Willie lifted the latch, the dog backed up a few steps and let Willie in the gate. Willie's twenty foot walk from the gate to the porch took three minutes and seven seconds. I couldn't tell he was moving. Maybe the dog couldn't either. If Willie could remember how he did it, the technique would be great for stalking deer.

Willie started to raise his hand to knock on the door, but the dog told him not to do it. He didn't actually say the words, but the message was relatively clear. His message was delivered by raising his upper lip. This time, he raised it far enough to show his teeth. As Willie's hand was raised, the dog's lip would move.

It was as though there was a string between Willie's hand and the dog's lip. Raise his hand a little, the lip moved a little. Move the hand some more, the lip rose a little more. The movements were so well tied together, that it was clear that by the time Willie touched the door, the dog's mouth would be around his wrist.

I blinked, and when I opened my eyes Willie was in the seat of the truck trying to convince me that nobody was home. At first I thought there were two Willies, but then I realized there was no longer one at the door of the house.

Unable to calm him down, I decided that I would check to see if anyone was home. The farm looked like it was too good of a hunting place to give up this easily. I should be able to get the job done. Dogs like me.

I was greeted at the gate just as Willie had been. The dog escorted me to the porch, and then he got between me and the door where Willie had attempted to knock. Because there were two doors on the porch, perhaps I could try the other one. Glancing at the dog, I checked to see if he had any objections. I raised my hand and his lip did not move. It was okay. I knocked several times, but nobody came to the door.

Having conditioned the dog to my presence, I figured that he would now permit a knock on the other door. I moved to the other door, and as I began to raise my hand, I noticed that an invisible string was now attached between my hand and the upper lip of the dog. As I moved my hand forward, the dog's lip would raise his lip to expose his perfectly white fangs. Retracting my arm would cause his lip to fall back to cover his teeth. Repeating this motion a few times was all I needed to convince myself that my hand could never make it all the way to the door frame.

Upon returning to the truck, I explained to Willie that nobody was home. It didn't matter anyway. On second glance, the farm didn't really look like it had that many deer on it anyway.

We spent the rest of the day hunting places and did finally get one lead that resulted in permission to archery hunt for deer. The owner and I became friends over the next few years, and I do still see him occasionally. He never told me why he gave us permission to hunt, so the mystery associated with obtaining permission still exists.

Finding a place to dove hunt can be just as frustrating as looking for any other type place. A lot of farmers must be afraid someone will shoot their wheat stubble and ruin it. I can't imagine what else could be hurt by dove hunters. At least, not if they are hunting a harvested field.

Willie and I decided to get back into dove hunting a few years ago. The quest for dove hunting spots had discouraged us a few years earlier, but we forgot enough about our frustrations that we were willing to try again.

We went about fifty miles west of where I live, and started asking permission. The corn crop on one huge farm had just been cut, so we stopped at the farmhouse to ask permission. The lady explained that she wouldn't let us hunt because some people from the village had hunted without permission. Pleading and whining didn't help. Complimenting her kids, promising to sign waivers, leaving a damage deposit, assuring her that we weren't village idiots, nothing worked.

Another farm had enough doves flying around to block out the sun for several seconds at a time. At the rate they were going onto the newly seeded pasture, there was no hope of growing any grass. Not unless something was quickly done to reduce the number of doves eating seed. We drove up to the farm house. The lady that came to the door looked like she was afraid of me. To make her feel more comfortable, I stepped back several feet from the door. This complicated matters because she was nearly deaf. After trying to calm her down, I explained that all I wanted was to get some of her doves.

As she slammed the door, I heard her saying, "No, I'm not interested in any young whipper snapper that wants some of my love." I learned to be careful about word choice when talking with people that have hearing problems. I'm one of those now, and it leads to some unusual conversations. People say the darndest things.

The small farm house across the street was in real bad shape, and a house trailer was at the side of it. Assuming that the house had been abandoned, I went to knock on the door of the house trailer. Nobody answered, so I went around back to check the work shed. Someone was in it working on a truck.

Willie and I walked back to the shed and interrupted the farmer that was working. He kind of growled and asked us what we needed. I'm sure that he had no idea because I had on a pair of jungle fatigues that I picked up while in the U.S. Air Force fifteen years earlier and Willie was wearing light weight camouflage clothes.

I told him that we were hoping to get to shoot a few doves, and would really appreciate getting to hunt.

"Where you two fellows from?"

Having grown up in the small town of Muckville, I knew better than to tell a farmer that I was from the city. Fortunately, I live in a suburb that is in a different county than the city. I gave him the name of the small town where I lived as a boy, then mentioned the name of the town where I currently lived and quickly explained the disappointment it was for me to be living so close to a city.

He squinted at me, and commented about the town being only slightly better than the city, but at least it wasn't the city itself. He then turned to Willie, and asked where he lived. Willie too had grown up in a small town, and he knew that he was in trouble because he lived in the same county as the city. He was able to refer to his suburb as a small town that permitted him to escape the city problems.

We were successful. Both of us disassociated ourselves from the city and showed genuine interest in being away from it. The farmer was convinced, and told us that we could hunt. He informed us that if we had been from the city, he would have chased us out. He said something about those city hunters having no respect for a farmer, his property, or his investment to farm the land.

It only took him an hour and a half to tell us a few of the reasons why he disliked the city, city people, and especially city hunters. We made a friend by listening to him, and actually got to hunt a place instead of just hunting places.

A Special Pot

RIVER COFFEE

There's something about waking early in the morning on a river bank and smelling a pot of coffee brewing on an open campfire. It makes it easier to get out of the sleeping bag and crawl from the tent. The smell of any pot of coffee will move most people from their beds, but a special blend of river coffee has a unique effect.

Many people make coffee while camping, even when on a river bank. Whether or not they make river coffee is not determined by where they camp but can only be ascertained from the methods they use to brew the coffee and the effect of the coffee on those who drink it.

Properly made river coffee has some fantastic properties. Those properties may be thoroughly enjoyed early in the morning, perhaps before breakfast. Another good time to enjoy river coffee is after the day's chores are all finished and everyone is sitting around the campfire thinking about the meaning of the day's events.

Good fishermen always spend some time together at the end of the day and reflect on the meaning of all that happened. Smart fishermen know that everything they do has a deeper meaning than simply working yourself to exhaustion to catch enough fish for the twenty family members that never wet a hook. Sometimes, at our campfire there would be a recounting of a special event from that day that should be forever etched in the memories of those present.

Fishing the Ohio River with a few close family members resulted in a simple observation. A person will go through a great deal of effort and hard work to experience the thrill of catching a big fish and to enjoy a simple pleasure such as drinking river coffee with friends and family. Nothing drank from a bottle or can could compare to the coffee we shared.

Making river coffee is a well-honed art to those people who know how to do it. In our fishing camp, there was one person who was recognized as the best at making river coffee. Everyone else was an understudy, hoping to someday be able to make coffee as good as our recognized expert.

Our expert used methods that may seem crude to the uninformed, or those that were never part of our circle. All that was needed was a tin coffee pot, water and coffee. Only one brand of coffee would do. No need for measuring cups or other such utensils. They just take up room in the equipment box and aren't needed.

My father was our expert coffee brewer when I was a boy. He learned the process when he was sixteen. His older brother Bob had been the teacher. Uncle Bob learned it from a seedy old fisherman that knew how to survive on a couple of dollars a week. Dad practiced the fine art of making river coffee for many years before I noticed it was anything special.

I was permitted to drink river coffee at a fairly young age, but I was about thirteen the first time that I noticed something uncommon was happening. We were on one of those special trips when neither my older brother nor Mom was with us. In fact, that particular summer had been filled with such trips, and Dad was beginning to share many special fishing and camping secrets with me.

It was getting to be evening and the campfire was already going. He offered to show me a special secret. I fetched a bucket of water for him, then he brought out the camping coffee pot that

I had seen so many times before. At one time it had been a percolator that Mom used on our gas stove back home. Now it was a river coffee pot. It was black most of the way up its sides from siting on past campfires.

Dad pulled the lid from the pot as he explained that he wanted to show me the way river men make their coffee. His brother and he made coffee in this manner for a couple of years while they fished the river to survive the Great Depression of the 1930s.

After the lid came off, he pulled out the coffee holder and the flanged tube that runs down inside all percolators. These items weren't needed when making river coffee. The pot was filled about three fourths full of water, then it was set on the grate which we had placed over the campfire. The grate was supported by four big rocks that we gathered prior to making the fire. It's a good idea to locate the rocks and make sure the grate will sit flat on them before a fire is built. At least there will be fewer skin burns if it is done in this sequence.

As the water came to a boil, a handful and a half of coffee grounds were thrown into the water. There was some kind of a transformation overtaking my father. His eyes changed a little and his voice became very serious as he explained that this recipe had come from his brother. I realized there was a link being made between me and my ancestry. My father was teaching me something that had been passed to him so that I could enjoy it and later pass it along to others. I could feel the moment was one of those special times to be remembered. I can't be exactly certain why I knew, but I did.

The coffee began to roll in the fast boil of the water, the water grew darker, and a light brown foam formed on the surface. The aroma was heavenly. It seemed that I may not need to drink any if I could just inhale this wonderful fragrance for a few minutes more. Soon, the pot was moved far enough to the side of the flame to permit the boiling to stop but still keep the coffee hot. After the boiling stopped, the coffee grounds settled to the bottom, and then two cups of coffee were carefully poured.

There was a brief suggestion that the coffee not be drank too fast. It was hot and might have a few grounds at the bottom of the cup. A special way to gently blow across the surface to cool the coffee was demonstrated and then a small sip taken from that upper layer of cooled coffee. The taste was a little stronger than the coffee made at home, but it was better. It was river coffee.

There were several minutes of silence as we sipped away. Each swallow warmed our bodies and souls as we strengthened the bond between a father and son. No coffee drank in a kitchen or diner could ever equal the effect of river coffee.

www.ingramcontent.com/pod-product-compliance
Lightning Source LLC
LaVergne TN
LVHW011348080426
835511LV00005B/198